God may not do ... ...he Bookless saga is a processic... ...ng barriers, repeatedly overridden by a prayer-answering God, often in unexpected ways. But this is far more than just one more heart-warming account of God's loving care for an individual family; it is a story of God's purposes being worked out in an apparently God-forsaken patch of west London, transforming in a literal sense a desolate wasteland into a garden. It spells out the human tensions and struggles in responding to the Bible mandates for creation care spelt out in Dave Bookless's first book, *Planetwise*. It tells us something about God's outworking of his plans through the Christian conservation organization A Rocha, encouraging each one of us on the way that he has a use for apparently improbable talents. And even better, it is very readable.

Professor Sam Berry, Department of Biology, University College London

For nearly two decades we have watched with admiration as Dave and Anne Bookless have applied their determined faith to the challenges of living in God's world in God's ways. Overcoming many painful obstacles with great courage, their commitments have led to the establishment of both an extraordinary project in one of London's more crowded and polluted boroughs and a growing movement for the care of creation throughout the UK. This honest and inspiring story of God's transformation within their own family and wider community encourages us all towards a deeper discipleship and an unshakeable hope.

Peter and Miranda Harris, Co-founders of A Rocha

In this deeply personal book, Dave Bookless shares his experience of God's love for this broken planet and for our broken lives. Through the pain of his own life experience, he is able to bring a message of the faithfulness of God and of the real meaning of Christian hope – with God, nothing is wasted.

Margot Hodson, an Anglican church pastor and previously Chaplain of Jesus College, Oxford. Margot is on the Boards of The John Ray Initiative and A Rocha UK. She and her husband Martin are the authors of Cherishing the Earth.

In this book you are invited to sit with a man who cares for the world we live in and the people we share the world with. He tells the story of his love of Jesus, his journey in faith and his journey of love with his wonderful Anne. Dave invites us in and shares with us both the glory and pain in life. We loved this book and would encourage anyone to buy it, because it's a book not just about A Rocha but about life and how to live it richly, day by day.
Mark and Lindsay Melluish, Senior Pastor and Assistant Pastor, St Paul's, Ealing

It's like finding a Martian who speaks English. Dave Bookless wakes us up to an appreciation and sense of responsibility for God's creation in such an engaging way. It's a great read by a fine storyteller.
Adrian Plass, author and broadcaster

A moving and highly personal account of success and suffering that will be particularly helpful to any Christian going through a dark period. This is both the story of the Bookless family and of the Christian environmental organization A Rocha, and it challenges us that part of Christian living is an environmentally sound lifestyle.

Are you depressed about the environmental crisis or about the trials of your personal family life? Then you will want to read this and see how God can intervene and use suffering and success to heal both people and the environment.
Professor Sir Ghillean Prance FRS, Chairman of A Rocha International

This story, both of A Rocha UK and of the 'Bookless Bunch', is wonderfully and movingly told. It brought tears to my eyes and inspired me in my desire to love God and look after all that he has made. Dave has been one of the pioneers in calling the church to pick up its mandate to take care of God's world, and it has been my privilege to work with him and learn from him. I have no hesitancy in encouraging you to read this book – you won't regret it!
Ruth Valerio, author of 'L' is for Lifestyle and manager of A Rocha UK's 'Living Lightly 24:1' project

GOD DOESN'T DO
WASTE

DAVE BOOKLESS

GOD DOESN'T DO
WASTE

REDEEMING THE WHOLE OF LIFE

ivp

INTER-VARSITY PRESS
Norton Street, Nottingham NG7 3HR, England
Email: ivp@ivpbooks.com
Website: www.ivpbooks.com

First published 2010

British Library Cataloguing in Publication Data
A catalogue record for this book is available from the British Library.

ISBN: 978–1–84474–473–2

Set in 11.5/14pt Chaparral
Typeset in Great Britain by CRB Associates, Potterhanworth, Lincolnshire
Printed and bound in Great Britain by Ashford Colour Press Ltd, Gosport, Hampshire

Inter-Varsity Press publishes Christian books that are true to the Bible and that communicate the gospel, develop discipleship and strengthen the church for its mission in the world.

Inter-Varsity Press is closely linked with the Universities and Colleges Christian Fellowship, a student movement connecting Christian Unions in universities and colleges throughout Great Britain, and a member movement of the International Fellowship of Evangelical Students. Website: www.uccf.org.uk

Contents

Acknowledgments and dedication

This book is a very personal reflection. While I have tried to represent situations and characters accurately and have checked details wherever possible, there may well be things that others remember differently. My apologies in advance to anybody I have inadvertently upset through omission or commission.

Similarly, although I would dearly love to thank each person who has been part of my life and of the A Rocha UK story for their unique and invaluable contributions, there simply isn't enough space. Moreover, books containing snippets about masses of individuals are interesting only if you know the people involved. A book of this length has to be very selective, and those mentioned are chosen because their stories illustrate and help the flow of the story.

I want to mention by name those who have helped directly in the writing of this book: from IVP Eleanor Trotter and Kath Stanton, and amongst friends and family commenting on various chapters or drafts: Rosemary Bookless (Mum), David and Beryl Bronnert, Colin Conroy, Richard Hall, Pete Hawkins, Sian Hawkins, Steve Hughes, Sarah Leedham, John and Jenny Simons, John Smiley, Richard Smillie and

Sarah Walker. Thank you all for your wise counsel and many helpful comments.

Most of all I want to thank, and dedicate this book to, my wife Anne and our daughters Hannah, Rebekah, Rosie and Naomi-Ruth, who have not only had to live with the story itself but with me as I've wrestled with how to tell it. Thank you for your encouragement, nourishment, distractions, sense of perspective and constant love. I can't put it better than St Paul: 'Every time you cross my mind, I break out in exclamations of thanks to God' (Philippians 1:3, *The Message*).

Dave Bookless
London
January 2010

Foreword

God Doesn't Do Waste is a fascinating title that resonated with me when I saw it, since I had recently received a beautiful pair of earrings made from recycled plastic bags found on a rubbish dump in one of the poorest areas of Peru, crafted by women living there. It was an illustration that God can make something beautiful out of what we call rubbish!

I knew nothing of the content of this book, but, as I read the first few chapters, I became excited as God's plan for Dave Bookless's life emerged.

Through a long sequence of events, including very difficult personal circumstances, Dave persisted in seeking God's way forward towards realizing his dream. He relates his journey from a distinct concern for the environment to the founding of A Rocha UK, a Christian nature conservation organization. He describes his involvement with A Rocha as a defining moment which brought together many of the threads of his life that had become important to him.

This book is challenging on many levels. It is easy to focus on successes, but while Dave is grateful to God for them, he is also honest about his struggles, the many family health issues, and the necessity of 'hanging in there' when prayers are not answered in the way he would have hoped. He and his wife Anne remain realistic in their understanding that God works through pain and suffering, as well as through healing.

God Doesn't Do Waste is eminently readable; it will raise the awareness of its readers that we can *all* do something to care for and preserve the beauty of God's world.

Fiona Castle

1 A load of rubbish: Scilly story

It is not my purpose to attempt a real autobiography. I simply want to tell the story of my experiments with truth . . . as my life consists of nothing but those experiments.[1]
M. K. Gandhi

It was, quite literally, a load of rubbish that changed my life. It was August 1989 and I was standing on the edge of a small cliff clutching several large plastic bags full of household waste, leaning forward to throw them over the edge. What happened next was not particularly dramatic, and at the time I certainly had no idea of its consequences, but my life's direction was to be altered as a result, and today I still find myself working through the implications.

The contents of those plastic bags summed up the previous two weeks: an idyllic holiday with my wife Anne and her parents. The bags were crammed with reminders of a fortnight's carefree living: fish and chip wrappers, wine bottles, tins, packaging and plastic trays. We'd been staying in a rented cottage on St Martin's in the Isles of Scilly. For those who don't know, the Scillies are twenty-five miles south-west of Land's End, a group of five small inhabited islands and several uninhabited ones, dotted around a shallow lagoon. They are famous for their mild climate ('sub-tropical paradise' according to the brochures), for spring flowers, rare birds and sandy beaches. We had spent a wonderful two weeks relaxing, swimming, birdwatching and reading, and of course plenty of eating and drinking too. When we came to clear up, we discovered we had accumulated a rather large heap of rubbish, and so we asked one of the islanders how to dispose of it all. The system has since changed, but back then we were simply told to burn the paper and card and to take any packaging, tins, bottles and plastics to 'the tip' at the end of the island.

With our full bin bags we walked across a picture-postcard view – springy rabbit-mown turf dotted with pink thrift flowers, wheeling gulls and near-empty sandy beaches, until we reached the end of the path. In front of us was a small cliff and below it a rocky bay containing 'the tip' – rusting tractors, mouldy cans, fragments of glass and multicoloured bits of plastic blowing about, with a few large, well-fed rats lazily ambling around. The contrast with our idyllic surroundings could not have been greater.

So there I was, standing on the clifftop with all our rubbish. As I silently added our wastefulness to the piles below, something unexpected happened. I sensed a voice speaking to me. The words were not audible but it was as if they resonated through every fibre of my body. What I heard was a simple question: 'How do you think I feel about what you're doing to my world?'

That question changed my life. I had always loved wildlife and beautiful places but had never given serious thought to the impact of my lifestyle on the planet. I had believed in a Creator God for as long as I could remember but had never taken any serious interest in environmental issues. Back then in 1989 nobody could have accused me of being a tree hugger! In fact I was pretty suspicious of the 'environmental movement', stereotyping it as full of slightly weird alternative people who worshipped the creation instead of the

Creator – Mother Earth rather than Father God. But as I stood on the clifftop on that beautiful August day, I knew at the core of my being that this was God speaking to me: 'How do you think I feel about what you're doing to my world?'

The implications whirled dizzily around my mind: God cares deeply about the mess that we've made of his beautiful fragile world; God is concerned about my behaviour, about the amount of waste I throw out, without thinking, week after week. My mind turned to my behaviour at home, every week putting the bin bags outside the front door and then promptly putting them out of my mind. I realized I had no idea what happened to the rubbish, yet now I dimly began to realize that God knew, and God cared about the anonymous landfill site where my rubbish joined everybody else's.

I had just completed my first year's training to be an Anglican vicar, studying theology at Trinity College, Bristol. In all my studies I had not heard anything about how God wants us to relate to the created world. Yet this experience was peeling back the cover of a whole can of theological worms. Who is this world for? What does my relationship with waste say about my relationship with God? How much do animals matter to God? Does God care about my lifestyle, or just about how I treat other people?

Of course not all these questions came to my mind immediately. What I experienced that summer's day was not so much a massive tectonic shift in my thinking and lifestyle, but rather the dislodging of a single stone that gradually gathers momentum and grows into an avalanche. However, as I stood under the pure blue sky, with the stillness of the green sea and the dazzling white of circling gulls, and looked down at the ugly, seeping wound of rubbish that I had just added to, I knew that something had to change.

This book is largely the story of all that has flowed from that moment. At one level it's about how one ordinary

British Christian family 'went green', and of the changes that have followed in terms of attitudes, lifestyle and even career. It is not meant to be an example to follow, both because each of us is so different, and also because I am certainly not a perfect role model – indeed, there are more examples to avoid than to imitate! At the same time, if this book encourages you to take risks, to step out of your comfort zone, to believe the world can be different and that you can be part of that change, then writing it will have been worthwhile.

At another level this is the story of a movement and of the organization that has birthed that movement, A Rocha UK, part of the wider global A Rocha family which seeks to care for God's fragile world in practical ways. It is a reflection on the joys and agonies of bringing a vision to birth, and of how that vision is shaped and modified through circumstances and the involvement of others. It is a story of God's call and how people have responded, and I have deliberately gone into some detail about how a very personal dream has developed into a team and an organization.

My family and I have received so much from our involvement with A Rocha, and if this book inspires others to get involved in what we believe is a wonderful movement of God, then I will be delighted.

Finally, in one sense this book isn't about the environment at all. It's a personal account of a life lived in relationship: an autobiography rather than an issue-based story. It is about roots and belonging, suffering and healing, identity and meaning, faith and doubt. It is about how in God's economy nothing need be wasted. As Archbishop Rowan Williams has put it: 'God doesn't do waste.' This is a story about the messiness that every human being wades through in every area of their lives, and a God who can take all that seems most wasteful and useless and recycle it into something of infinite worth.

2 Roots and rootlessness

To be rooted is perhaps the most important and least recognized need of the human soul.[1]
Simone Weil, French-Jewish philosopher, 1909–1943

I have never really felt like I was 'from' anywhere . . . I speak with the accent of nowhere – the accent of a person who has no fixed home in their mind.[2]
Douglas Coupland, *Life After God*

It is a very long way from the peaceful and pretty Isles of Scilly to the human whirlpool – and sometimes cesspool – of urban Kolkata, but that is where my life's story begins. Calcutta, as it was still known when I was born there, is one of the largest cities in India, with a population of over fifteen million. It is a place of astonishing contradictions and tensions: poverty and wealth, Hinduism and Islam, despair and joy, unbridled capitalist entrepreneurship alongside an elected communist government. Calcutta has inspired the heights of human achievement in Bengali poetry, art, music, architecture and film, yet it is also a place where subhuman indifference to suffering and disability are visible on every street corner. It is both the city of Mother Theresa, the icon of human compassion, and of Mata Kali, seen by many as the terrifying goddess of destruction. Of course I was unaware of all this when my parents moved to Calcutta in 1961, and I entered the world a few months later.

My parents, Guy and Rosemary, were committed Christians; so committed in fact that they had each gone to India, turning their backs on career opportunities in post-war England, and responding to a sense of God's call to serve local people and share the love of Jesus Christ. They each imagined that this might close the door on opportunities of marriage and children. My father even contemplated joining a semi-monastic brotherhood. However, their mission agency posted them both to Patna in the dusty, poverty-stricken North Indian state of Bihar. There they met and fell in love. In many ways it was a marriage of opposites. The gentle, balding, academic clergyman with an impeccable public school and Cambridge background was won over by the spirited, younger schoolteacher and gardener's daughter from the Midlands. Although they worked together as colleagues, it was only on a holiday in Kashmir with other missionaries that romance could blossom. Even after their engagement, local culture decreed that private meetings had to take place on the open veranda of the mission house. They returned to England to marry in April 1961 before setting sail for a new joint posting in Calcutta, where Guy was to lecture in theology at Bishop's College.

My mother was in her mid-thirties and my father over forty when they married, so perhaps it was no surprise that they were quick off the mark in starting a family. I entered the world ten months to the day after my parents' wedding, on 22 February 1962. My memories of those first few years are inevitably coloured by old photographs and the retelling of stories, but I am reliably informed that I was a lively and noisy toddler who raced around the leafy grounds of Bishop's College making friends with all the students.

While my parents both worked and studied, I was looked after by a wonderful local 'ayah' or nanny. As a result, my very first words were in Hindi and Bengali. Sadly I cannot remember any of them now, because we left Calcutta in 1965, after my father's health collapsed. However, in another sense, Calcutta and the North Indian languages have never left me. Overhearing a Hindi conversation, smelling Indian street-food, standing in a bustling multiracial overcrowded urban area, stir very deep memories, and probably have a lot to do with where I have decided to live and what I have chosen to do ever since.

Leaving Calcutta also started what has become a recurring theme for much of my life: being uprooted and moved from one place to another at frequent intervals. Bearing in mind that I was conceived in Britain before my parents set sail for Calcutta, travel has been in my blood since before my birth. When we arrived in freezing England in 1965, we spent a year moving from one temporary house to another, while my parents spoke at churches around the country about the joys and needs of India. Little did any of us know that one of the places we lived, Nailsea, near Bristol, would become the home of my future wife, or that Holy Trinity Church, which I attended aged four, would also witness my wedding many years later. By this time I had a little brother, Andy, almost eighteen months younger than me, so at least there was someone to play with, but still it was a time of constant disturbance and change, with nowhere really to call home. Eventually CMS, the Church Missionary Society, which my parents were working with, found a placement for us in a part of India that had a much healthier climate than Calcutta: the then 'garden city' of Bangalore. So in 1966 we moved to the United Theological College, with its spacious campus and international blend of students and staff.

We lived in Bangalore for six largely happy years. My father lectured, and my mother did further study and some teaching. My brother and I went to school, and I grew from a lively four-year-old to a somewhat tearaway ten-year-old. To me, the college campus was effectively a large outdoor playground, and I had the run of it. It was very safe, apart from the occasional cobra, and the international group of resident staff children made a semi-feral gang, racing around on bicycles or on foot, climbing trees, shooting catapults at snakes and squirrels, and pestering the students for stamps from their various home countries.

When I was seven, my parents took me out of the local English medium school in Bangalore, where I was very happy, and sent me to Lushington Hall, a missionary boarding school (now called Hebron), two hundred miles away in the Nilgiri Hills. They were doing what everybody agreed was best to prepare me academically and culturally for a future return to the UK. It was also a deeply Christian school, which they knew would give me good spiritual foundations. But it was hard to leave friends, home, and the freedom of the college campus for a strange, cold boarding school 6,000 feet up in the mountains where I didn't know anybody. For the first time in my life I was profoundly unhappy for a while, with a sense of being painfully uprooted from all that was most important to me.

As I've looked back, I have realized this was also the time when I first began to explore the natural world. Once a week, on Sunday afternoons, all the pupils were made to sit in silence at desks and write letters home. A few years ago my mother dug out a keepsake box in which she'd preserved some of my first letters. They were full of drawings and descriptions of birds, animals and insects that I'd seen in the well-wooded school compound. Although I could never have expressed it then, I was instinctively drawn to God's creation at a time when I was lonely and unsettled. Like Elijah, Isaiah, Jonah and Job in the Bible, I found God's still small voice speaking to me through the beauty and complexity of nature.

In 1972, when I was ten, we returned to England. My parents felt that their elderly parents needed them. They also wanted my brother and me to adapt to the British education system before we were teenagers. It was another deeply unsettling time. While my father spent a term lecturing in Cambridge and then looked for a job as a vicar, my mother struggled to come to terms with how England had changed while she'd been away. I have a vivid memory of the embarrassment of being dragged around a super-market by a mum who hadn't really grasped the concept of trolleys and self-service and kept asking the staff to fetch things for her. At least she didn't try to haggle over the price as we would have done in India!

Meanwhile I was finding England fairly bewildering too. Compared with India, the pace of life seemed so fast, and the climate and the people so cold. I was probably a slightly strange ten-year-old. It was 1972, but I had never listened to a pop song in my life. We had no radio or television in India, and I had never heard of Elvis, the Rolling Stones, or even the Beatles until long after they'd disbanded. Worst of all, I had an accent that was an odd mixture of British and Indian. Although I put a brave face on it and tried to lose my accent and fit in, I was deeply unhappy and desperately missed the sights, sounds and smells of India, as well as the friends and familiar toys I'd left behind. India had entered my psycho-logical and emotional bloodstream, and although I would spend many years trying to suppress it and to fit in as a young Briton, India would inevitably bubble up again further downstream.

A legacy from my grandfather meant my parents could just about afford to send my brother and me to boarding school. They wanted us to have the best education, a nurturing Christian environment and some stability after so much upheaval, so we were sent to Monkton Combe School, just outside Bath. At the junior school I was very self-conscious about my Indian accent. I would try to impress my classmates by messing about in lessons or allowing myself to be talked into crazy escapades around the school. Usually I only succeeded in digging myself into an even deeper hole and looking silly. This culminated in an infamous occasion when I was thirteen and we were sitting mock exams.

The school still used old-fashioned fountain pens, and each classroom had an inkwell to refill them. Somebody suggested that putting oil in each of the inkwells would cause all the pens in the school to jam during the exams. My inner anarchist was inspired and I saw the chance to make my mark. One evening I crept around the classrooms adding oil to the inkwells, got caught, and inevitably found myself in big trouble. Amazingly I escaped the cane; perhaps the headmaster realized I'd been put up to it, but my punishment was to sit lots of extra exam papers in my free time. This backfired somewhat when it came to the actual exams, as all the extra practice meant that I did far better than anybody expected, and sailed through the entrance exams for Monkton Combe Senior School. However, my three years at Monkton Junior were not a great success. The final report from the headmaster summed it up: 'I feel we have failed with Bookless. Perhaps if we had had longer it would have been different.'

It was around this time that my parents encouraged me to spend a week of the summer holidays at a boys' Christian holiday camp by the Dorset seaside in Swanage. Like many young teenagers, I was at something of a spiritual cross-roads. While I had never doubted God's existence, and went regularly to church with my parents and to chapel at school, I found it all somewhat boring and disconnected from reality. My experience of life thus far had done little to convince me that God was really bothered with me. However the Christian camp made me think again. I was surrounded by young people of my own age and slightly older who were committed Christians. There was a huge amount of high-energy fun, with games and trips and lots of food. Most of the leaders were students: bright, likeable, game for a laugh, and yet very clear about what they believed and why. One evening the camp's senior leader, John Eddison, gave a talk based around William Holman Hunt's famous painting, *The Light of the World*, and the verse on which it is based, Revelation 3:20. He showed us a copy of the picture, with Jesus holding a lantern, standing in the dark knocking at an overgrown door. He explained that this represented the door to each of our inner lives. Jesus was saying, 'Behold! I stand at the door and knock.' He wanted to come in, to befriend and forgive and help us. Then John Eddison pointed out that there was no handle on the outside of the door. Jesus was not going to force his way in. It was up to each of us to decide whether or not to open the door and invite him in.

That evening I realized that I didn't have to keep trying to live up to other people's expectations. I became newly aware that God knew me; he knew all about my thoughts and feelings, accepted and loved me, and wanted to be in my life. Back in my dormitory, I quietly invited Jesus to come in, to remove the insecurity and loneliness in my life, and to take control of my destiny. That evening I moved from being a child raised in a Christian family to having a Christian commitment of my own. Of course I didn't have a clue about what I was really letting myself in for; I just knew I wanted Jesus to be part of it.

It would be convenient to write that this new Christian commitment made things easier when I started Monkton Senior School. Instead things got worse. Many of my junior school contemporaries arrived at the same time as me, and so I came with a reputation for being 'a bit of a prat'. Worse, the school was divided into houses, and I ended up in one with a fairly nasty group of bullies in the years above me. I was characterized by the unfortunate combination of being small for my age but with a big mouth and the tendency to open it too often. Soon I was picked on, and on several occasions physically bullied quite severely. There is nothing more likely to damage somebody psychologically than persistent abuse, and I began to shrivel up in terms of confidence and friendships.

But, as in India, I turned to the natural world and went for long walks, exploring the extensive school grounds and the valley of the Midford Brook and River Avon. I started to learn the names and habits of local wildlife, discovering where the badgers' setts were and which parts of the river contained lurking trout or pike. In particular I took delight in birdlife: in the variety of colours, shapes, songs and behaviour, and in the miracles of flight and migration. I kept lists of what I saw and when: sand martins that nested in a sandy bank of the Midford Brook, migrating to Africa and back each year; plump black and white dippers bobbing on stones in the river and swimming underwater to catch aquatic insects; long-tailed tits, tiny balls of pink, white and black fluff flitting in groups through the woods with their twittering calls, and of course the elusive but spectacular kingfisher piercing the stillness with its sharp contact call and flash of iridescent blue-green-orange. In the otherness of nature, I was able to escape from the bullying and stresses of school and find my own place in observation and in stillness.

My recent commitment to Christ also meant that I did not feel as alone as before. I knew deep down, even when I didn't feel it, that God cared for me personally. However, at the time I never made any coherent links between my growing personal faith and the way the natural world was feeding my soul so deeply. Jesus was so personal, so intimate to me in my prayer life and my Bible reading, that I couldn't really relate to him also being Lord of Creation. That was just too big for me to comprehend.

With the advantage of hindsight, I can also see that the teaching I received in churches, through books and in the school Christian Union focused almost exclusively on 'spiritual' aspects of Christian faith. Prayer, reading the Bible, enjoying fellowship with other Christians, and sharing Jesus with others, were seen as the only *really* Christian activities. It was all about a personal decision, a personal relationship, and a commitment to getting others on board, so that they too could end up in the same destination – a heaven somewhere 'way beyond the blue horizon' – and certainly nothing to do with this earth down here. We might talk about God as Creator and sing 'O Lord my God, when I in awesome wonder Consider all the works Thy hand hath made', yet there was no concept that Jesus had anything to do with wildlife, the seasons or the environment as a whole.

Eventually the bullies in the year above either grew up, split up, left, or in a couple of cases were expelled when other misdemeanours were discovered. I took part in sport, music and drama activities that built my confidence. I also began to grow in my faith, nurtured by the school's active Christian Union and by Widcombe Baptist Church in nearby Bath, to which a group of us would go on a Sunday evening. We went partly for the worship and teaching, but also because a youth group that included girls was a very attractive proposition to the inmates of an all-male boarding school.

By the time I reached the sixth form I had changed considerably from the mixed-up kid who had arrived at Monkton Combe. I had acquired a good group of friends, was enjoying my A levels, and was beginning to express my Christian faith through helping in a local village Sunday school and fundraising for projects in Africa. When I left Monkton, it was with three good A levels and, to everybody's surprise, a place to read history at Jesus College, Cambridge the following year. I also had a growing confidence in my faith and in the person that God had made me.

Before going to Cambridge, I spent nine months based at my parents' home, which at that time was in the tiny village of Wysall, south of Nottingham, where my father was vicar of three churches. For the first time in my life I obtained a job to earn some money, doing clerical work in the nearby Institute of Geological Sciences in Keyworth. I got involved in the nearest lively church youth group at East Leake, as well as helping to run several children's missions and holiday clubs in my dad's churches and elsewhere around the East Midlands. In the summer I undertook my first independent travel, going to Frankfurt in Germany to see something of a different European culture.

In October 1980 I began four years of university life in the beautiful city of Cambridge, with its rich history and bizarre ancient traditions. Jesus College was both central and surrounded by green fields. This was a wonderful and hugely privileged time. For most of my first three years I did the minimum necessary to keep up with course work. I would attend lectures (usually) and supervisions (regularly) and hand in my essays on time (just about) – even when it meant staying up to do a week's work in one night. It wasn't that I didn't find modern history interesting, but rather that Cambridge simply had so much more to offer. I tried out a wide range of the clubs and societies available, having a go at athletics and drama, joining the India Society and the Cambridge Bird Club, taking up squash and barbershop singing. Along with two friends, I founded a new society – no more weird and wonderful than many others at the time – called CUSTODY, the Cambridge University Society for the Tasting of Diverse Yogurts. We had termly themed yogurt-tasting events, including a yogurt Olympics (haven't you heard of the 110m curdles?), and invented dozens of new flavours (Marmite and smoked mackerel are especially memorable, though not for the best reasons). Our chief claim to fame was getting mentioned on Radio 1 and in *The Times* in the same week.

I also threw myself into Christian activities, trying out all the livelier local churches, each with their own particular flavour, some with contemporary music, others with long but helpful sermons. I joined a small Christian choir, the Ichthyan Singers, and attended a midweek, late-night, informal Eucharist in Jesus College Chapel which had a timeless beauty to it. I also frequented and eventually led the Church Mission Society group, linking me back to my parents' work in India.

Most of all, I got involved in the student Christian Union, with Bible study groups in the college and weekly talks organized through the CICCU (the Cambridge Inter-Collegiate Christian Union). Hundreds of students would gather for Saturday night Bible readings, where well-known Christian speakers, many of them superb communicators, took a Bible passage and explained its meaning and relevance for up to an hour. On Sunday evenings we would gather again for evangelistic meetings, to which we were encouraged to bring our student friends. Within Jesus College we saw the number of those who considered themselves committed Christians grow steadily, as many students took the opportunity and freedom of university life to consider the big questions of life's meaning and purpose. I was thrilled to be a small part of this, and to see good friends I'd made – some of whom were far more intelligent than me – weigh up the evidence for God's existence and for the astounding claim that Jesus is God-with-us, and then decide to follow him themselves. Some of the friendships have remained ever since.

My interest in India was also reawakened at Cambridge, although the process had already begun when I studied

E. M. Forster's *A Passage to India* as one of my A Level English set texts. Forster's evocative descriptions of India's landscape, climate and cultures awakened in me a latent nostalgia for my childhood home. In addition, his criticism of the 'poor, little, talkative Christianity' he saw when exported English religion confronted the long spiritual history of India struck a deep chord. I was becoming aware that God was so much bigger than my experience of him and the Westernized cultural expressions of Christianity I had encountered. Studying modern history at Cambridge, I chose options looking at India and Africa in the struggle for independence, and then a unit on Gandhi's influence on Indian politics. I spent week after week in the university library, devouring Gandhi's writings: his autobiography, the wonderfully named *Story of my Experiments with Truth*, his speeches, and the opinions his contemporaries formed of him. I was struck by his criticism of much missionary work and of Western Christendom: 'Western nations today are groaning under the heel of the monster-god of materialism.'[3] Yet Gandhi was also deeply attracted by the person of Jesus Christ, and was possibly more influenced by the Sermon on the Mount than by any other single piece of scripture of any faith. His closest friend was the missionary C. F. Andrews, nicknamed 'Christ's Faithful Apostle' (CFA) for the simple Christlikeness of his lifestyle. As I read more about Gandhi, I was haunted by his words, 'I like your Christ. I do not like your Christians. Your Christians are so unlike your Christ.'[4]

My reaction to this was not to reject my Christian faith, but to recognize how important it was not to limit that faith to a particular culture and language. I could see so much that was good in non-Western cultures, and in many of the lives and teachings within other faiths. I found it difficult to reconcile this with the views of some of my Christian friends, who saw anybody who wasn't a follower of Jesus as hopelessly 'lost in darkness', and other religions as totally 'of the devil'. For years I struggled to hold together my commitment to the Bible and Jesus' clearly exclusive claims to be 'the way, the truth and the life' with the devout spirituality that I saw in people such as Gandhi, and later in my Hindu, Sikh and Muslim friends.

Eventually it was, yet again, an understanding of God as Creator that helped me integrate these tensions. If we focus solely on Jesus as Saviour, we can become unnecessarily narrow in our opinion of people who have not accepted him. However, when we recognize that the Bible presents Jesus as Creator and Sustainer as well as Saviour, then we can see signs of God's love, grace, creativity and truth within everything and everyone that God has made. An inadequate theology of creation may lead to seeing people in a less than godly way, merely as targets for conversion rather than uniquely precious individuals who bear God's image.

India was by now calling me strongly. In the summer of 1982 I returned, ten years after leaving as a child. I went with a student friend, David Lewis, whose geography degree entailed a research project for which he chose the suitably obscure topic 'The Electrification of Rural Villages in Madurai District'. This was partly because another friend, Philip Swan, was based at a Christian college in Madurai and offered to find us accommodation.

My own motives for revisiting India were multiple. It was to be a personal journey in re-examining my roots, and tracking down some of the people and places that had shaped my childhood. It was also the classic student back-packer exploration of a wider world: nine weeks travelling thousands of miles by second-class train or local bus, visiting most of India's big cities (Delhi, Mumbai, Chennai, Kolkata, Bangalore), taking in both tourist sites such as the Taj Mahal, and places of spiritual significance such as the pilgrim city of Varanasi and the enormous Meenakshi Temple in

Madurai. At the same time it was a spiritual journey in terms of the questions of Christian faith and Indian culture that had begun to fascinate me. I was keen to look more deeply at what it meant to be truly Indian and truly Christian – to seek tangible examples of how Christianity was taking root in Indian soil.

Unusually for me, I kept a detailed journal throughout the trip to India. Just before setting off I observed:

> Cultures, unlike the gospel, are constantly changing and developing organisms, and Christ will only enrich the good within them and winnow out the bad . . . That then is the theory, and in India I intend to observe and assess how it has been worked out in widely varying contexts. I go, not really knowing what I will find, and I see this as an advantage in that I cannot prejudge. I go to probe and to listen and, I hope, to learn. It will, I am aware, prove a challenge to my sheltered faith, and yet I know it is necessary to prevent me from entering a realm of words without actions, of faith without experience.

India lived up to all my expectations and exploded many of my preconceptions. I was exposed to dirt, poverty and chaos that I had been protected from as a child; to the bitter hopelessness of caste and the cynical corruption of power that pervade the subcontinent and have sadly seeped into the churches. At the same time, David Lewis and I experienced innumerable acts of selfless kindness and unassuming hospitality, and were awed by India's rich history, philosophy and architecture. We spent time in village chai shops, dusty railway stations, big cities and, whenever we could, people's homes, listening to Hindus, Sikhs, Muslims, Indian Christians and Western missionaries. We visited temples, ashrams,[5] colleges and schools, soaking ourselves in what it meant to wrestle with faith and culture in an Indian context.

India is full of extraordinary contradictions, from the obvious dynamics of wealth and poverty, barrenness and plenty, chaos and peace, to the subtler tensions between deep spirituality and crass materialism, or of sitting on a long-distance train talking to an ordinary-looking dhoti-clad man who turns out to be a nuclear physicist describing himself as a Hindu atheist.

Our experience of Indian Christianity is impossible to distil into a few sentences or stories. Rather, I've looked at my journals and selected, almost at random, one hot day in late July 1982. It was a day of two contrasting encounters. We were staying in the temple city of Tiruchirappalli with a Tamil Christian, Revd Gnanaiah, and his family. Through the morning we had long conversations about Tamil culture and Christian faith. Gnanaiah was an accomplished Tamil poet who believed that Christianity in India should always be expressed in the language, music, clothing and architecture that have shaped the landscape and people for thousands of years. He was adamant that missionaries had done a terrible disservice by associating Christianity so closely with Western culture. In his youth, Gnanaiah had even been a radical Indian nationalist, joining groups setting fire to 'imperialist' buildings. Yet he was also clear that Christ must challenge his own culture, and uncompromising in his belief that caste and many other Hindu customs were incompatible with following Jesus. He spent his life in rural Tamil Nadu, training others to sit under the trees in each village and tell stories of Jesus.

Later that same day I caught a bus to visit somewhere with a totally different perspective on Christ in India, the Shanti Vanam (Wilderness of Peace) Ashram founded by the Roman Catholic Bede Griffiths. The ashram occupied an idyllic spot on the banks of the slow-flowing Cauvery river. It was laid out in traditional Hindu style, with shady glades and a central chapel based on South Indian temples containing a central gopuram (tower) covered in carved statues. Most visitors were Westerners with straggly beards and sadhu's robes. One had just returned from forty days of silent meditation in a Himalayan cave. As I sat cross-legged with him under a tree, he explained that he believed faith and culture were so deeply intertwined that no Westerner could ever really become a Hindu, nor any Indian truly become a Christian. I was impressed by his asceticism, but choked on my sweet chai at his words. He was effectively saying that it was all right for him as a Westerner to flirt with Indian spirituality, and at Shanti Vanam to worship in a temple where the Christian Trinity were carved in the form of Hindu deities, and a phallic Shiva lingam occupied the place usually taken by a cross. Yet he withheld the right of Indians to discover the riches to be found in Christ. What did this say to the Indian church which has existed since the first century when the apostle Thomas visited Kerala and Tamil Nadu, long before Christianity reached Britain? What did his attitude say to those Indians who risked losing homes, jobs, families, and sometimes even their lives, in order to follow Jesus? It was one of my first encounters with the intolerance that dresses itself as liberal pluralism. Later in our trip we would also discover the rising Hindu funda-mentalist nationalism, which welcomes Christ as long as he is seen as simply another Hindu deity, but is strongly, often violently, opposed to the freedom to choose one's own religion.

Returning from India, I threw myself into my final year of undergraduate studies with belated enthusiasm. The year passed in a blur of reading, essays, revision and exams, interspersed with parties and May balls. As my friends began to apply for jobs in the City and industry, or to do further training as lawyers or doctors, I found that India had helped me narrow down my potential career choices. I was very aware of the privileged opportunities that my background had afforded me, with a loving family, education at Monkton and Cambridge, and wonderful Christian nurturing both in India and in the UK.

Jesus' words in Luke 12:48 kept returning to my mind. It's a verse that, as time has gone on and I have become more aware of our misuse of the earth's resources and the injustice of our overconsumption, has continued to echo in my mind ever more loudly: 'From everyone who has been given much, much will be demanded; and from the one who has been entrusted with much, much more will be asked.'

3 Teaching and learning in Bradford and Devon

There was this old definition of generosity, which is [that] at the very least the rich man looks after the poor man on his street. Guess what? Now that street goes round the globe.[1]
Bono from U2

What was I to do next? I wanted more than anything to serve God to the best of my ability, but the questions were 'how?' and 'where?'. It would have been convenient to receive a blinding revelation from heaven, but I was discovering that God usually guides through less dramatic methods: thinking things through, reading the Bible and prayerfully listening to others. As I did so, I reckoned there were three possible areas God was calling me into: serving the church in India, ordination to become a vicar in the Church of England, or work with children and young people, perhaps teaching. While I was drawn to go back to India immediately, I was advised to get some more training and experience first. Ordination was something I didn't yet feel ready for, although I had been stimulated by opportunities to preach while in India. Therefore I decided to spend the next year training as a teacher, which would be good preparation for any of the three longer-term options.

So began a fourth year in Cambridge, studying for a post-graduate certificate in education. I chose religious education as my main subject, as the course offered the chance to look at several major world faiths, and I had previously studied only Christianity and Hinduism in any depth. My fellow students were a friendly and extremely diverse group, including a Jew, a Buddhist, a smattering of Christians of various traditions, and a couple of convinced atheists. I revelled in the challenge of relating my Christian beliefs both to the teachings of other faiths, and to the individuals I got to know. I found then, as I have since, that spending time understanding and relating to those of other beliefs did not undermine my Christian faith, but rather caused it to become more focused, less flabby and ultimately much stronger. I also found the teacher training course much more relevant to real life than most of my undergraduate studies. Although somewhat nervous to begin with, I learned to relish the challenge of teaching practice in secondary schools near Cambridge, finding creative ways to get bored teenagers interested in how the major religions answer life's big questions.

All too soon it was time to look for a teaching job. I was sure that I wanted to work in a multiracial and multifaith urban school. I knew this would be challenging, but at least I reckoned there would be less competition for the jobs! Then, as since, I've found it strange that so many Christians, while being theoretically prepared to go wherever God calls them, seem equally as likely as non-Christians to incline towards applying for more comfortable places to live and work. As the vicar of an inner-city parish once said to me, 'Why is it that God seems to be calling all the Christians to live in suburbia?'

I sent off a few applications, and the first interview I was offered was in a middle school for 9–13s in Bradford, teaching religious education and a mix of other subjects. As the train pulled into the station and I saw Bradford for the first time, terraced streets sprawling messily up the hillsides around the Aire valley, I had a totally unexpected but very clear sensation that I was coming home, that this was indeed where God wanted me for the next stage of my life. The interview was at a huge square Victorian brick box of a building with more than a passing resemblance to Colditz castle. The job wasn't quite what the advertisement had suggested: it was to include a third of a timetable of RE, with another third music and the rest a mix of history and geography. I hadn't studied geography since I was fourteen, and as for music, my only qualifications were a few piano lessons, self-taught guitar and membership of various amateur choirs.

I was also less than impressed with the atmosphere in the school. The staffroom was deeply stained, not just with nicotine but with the resentment of teachers who'd become stuck in their prejudices but had nowhere else to go. The head, with his bow tie and Brylcreemed hair, cut a strange figure in a school where 90% of the pupils were of conservative Pakistani Muslim background. Despite my reservations, when I was offered the job I accepted immediately, confident that this was where God wanted me.

So Bradford became my home for four formative years. The contrast to Cambridge could not have been greater. Moving from a rarefied atmosphere of privilege and wealth, I now found myself in a gritty former mill town, struggling with post-industrial issues of unemployment and lack of opportunity in Thatcher's Britain. Whereas in Cambridge different cultures and faiths meant opportunities to stretch horizons and enrich understanding, in Bradford such differences meant threat and competition. The city seemed composed of two monolithic conservative working-class cultures, white Yorkshire and Pakistani Muslim, each highly suspicious of the other. Whether through economic hardship, lack of education, or cultural conservatism, 'the other' was to be treated with suspicion.

I was shocked to see how far this attitude had extended into the churches. On one occasion I spoke to a women's group about mission and Christianity in India. I put together a slideshow (no PowerPoint in 1985!), starting with classic views of the Taj Mahal, wildlife, bustling cities and poor villages. I went on to talk about Indian Christianity and the challenges of getting rid of the baggage of Empire and 'Britishness' to find an Indian Jesus. I had their interest up to this point, and they asked good questions about how they could support and pray for Christians in India. But then I changed tack and started slipping in pictures of mosques and gurdwaras, surrounded not by the dust of India, but by the old mills and churches of Bradford, slides of 'Bombay Stores', and of Muslim children heading off to their madrasas on Otley and Barkerend Road. I started to hint that mission was not just about 'over there', but about welcoming the 'foreigners' when they were our near neighbours.

It was as if I had lanced a festering boil as unbridled prejudice and racism were unleashed. The masks of respectability and polite interest were removed, and replaced by torrents of question and accusation: 'Why are *they* here?', 'What are they doing in *our* country?', 'They don't behave like us . . . don't fit in . . . They should go home!'

I found similar attitudes in the schools. At the school where I worked I could hardly bear to enter the staffroom, where resentment and racism were openly, even proudly, displayed. Instead I would sit in an empty classroom, sharing sandwiches and samosas with the school's only Muslim teacher and one other colleague, discussing how we could subvert the values we found around us. In the mid-1980s, before the uniformity of Ofsted and the national curriculum, there was freedom for teachers to be creative, and my history lessons gradually moved from Roman Britain and the kings of England to the Mughals in India and the history of relations between Britain and the subcontinent. In music, I discovered that in the vast majority of local Muslim homes there was no musical tradition at all, so, abandoning the suggested teaching of 'English Country Garden', I asked the children to bring in tapes of anything they had at home. Mostly these were simple Urdu or Arabic rhymes, teaching the alphabet or reciting favourite passages from the Koran. Then I tried a different tack, looking at the lyrics of popular songs and how they often reflected the big issues of the time. The children became animated and energized at the idea of writing protest songs. Before long they were composing their own, an experiment that had to come to a rapid halt when the main subject of protest became the headteacher and his oppressive regime!

My contract ended after a year, and I applied for another post down the valley in Keighley. Here there was a greater ethnic mix, the staff were less jaundiced, and the atmosphere was healthier. However, the same attitudes lurked close to the surface in the local community. In RE I was following the new Bradford agreed syllabus which covered the five major faiths found in the city: Christianity, Islam, Sikhism, Hinduism and Judaism. After one inoffensively factual lesson on Islam, I was summoned to the head's office to be faced with a fuming parent. 'Why are you teaching this foreign rubbish to my daughter? I only want her to learn about the English religion!' Stung by her attitude, and also by the complicity of the head in allowing such open prejudice to go without comment, I asked with just a tinge of sarcasm: 'Oh, the English religion – and which one might that be?' She turned red. 'Are you taking the mick? The English religion – about Jesus and Mary and that.' 'Ah, I see . . . well unfortunately that's not the English religion. You see, Jesus Christ was an Asian, and Christianity is more an Asian religion than an English one. The only religion England has actually produced is the pre-Christian pagan religion to do with Druids, summer solstices and worshipping trees and rivers and . . . Is that what you want your daughter to learn?' 'Don't be stupid! You know perfectly well what I mean.' 'Yes I do. You want your daughter to learn about the Christian faith, and so do I because I'm a committed Christian myself. At the same time, we live in a city with many different religions, and Bradford's agreed syllabus rightly insists that pupils should understand what other religions believe too. If you want your daughter to learn more deeply about the Christian faith, I suggest you take her to church.' At this point the head finally stepped in, realizing that things were getting somewhat heated: 'Thank you Mrs Ryan, both you and Mr Bookless have made your points. I will continue to monitor the situation closely.'

That incident was one of many where issues of faith and culture came to the fore, both at work and in church. I realized how my childhood in India and my struggles to adapt to Britain, even my experience of bullying, were not wasted, but were being used by God to make me more cross-culturally sensitive. I had the perspective to see English culture critically, both as shaped by Christianity, and also as affected by forces that worked against Christian values.

When I heard that Bradford Council had opened an Interfaith Education Centre to help teachers cope with the new multifaith syllabus, and were looking for a Christian staff member, I was intrigued. Initially the centre had been staffed with Muslim, Sikh, Hindu and Jewish lecturers, as the local authority expected that teachers would need help in understanding and teaching these 'new' faiths. However, after a year, they discovered that there was an equal need to help teachers present Christianity, not as 'the English religion' but rather as a diverse and vibrant world faith. I applied for the post as lecturer in Christianity as a world religion, was interviewed and appointed.

What an opportunity: the chance to help shape how Christianity was presented in schools across the whole local authority! Quickly I discovered just how sketchy most non-specialist RE teachers' knowledge of the Christian faith was, so I set about running workshops and writing a series of booklets for teachers. One, *What Do Christians Believe?*, was written to cover all the key doctrines that different denominations hold in common, and I was able to get church leaders from all the major local churches to endorse it. Ten years after leaving Bradford, I had a letter from the local authority, which was still using the booklet and wanted my permission to update and revise it.

Beyond workshops and writing, schools were desperate for audio-visual resources, so a borrowed video camera and some very amateur editing led to clips of worship from a whole range of local churches that could be shown in RE lessons. In addition, I raided the resources of Christian agencies working overseas to beg for or borrow pictures and stories of worship in India and Pakistan, South America, Africa and the Far East. I was keen to show Christianity as global, lively, growing and wonderfully varied. I was also determined to do all in my power to destroy the damage done by the false idea that late twentieth-century Britain, in its moral confusion and crass consumerism, was somehow a 'Christian' country, or that racial or cultural prejudice had any place in the Christian faith.

Throughout my time in Bradford I was increasingly involved in a local church, St Augustine's on Otley Road. When I arrived in 1984 it was a great barn of a Victorian building, with a robed choir that sometimes almost out-numbered the smallish congregation. However the vicar, Robin Gamble, was anything but traditional. With his gingery-fair hair, beard, colourful glasses, and even more colourful turn of phrase, Robin smashed into smithereens the mould of what a vicar should be. He was Bradford through-and-through, passionate about the football club, but even more passionate about making Jesus come alive to local people. I threw myself into helping with the emerging worship group and work among teenagers, as Robin's preaching and personality began to attract more people. I ended up sharing a flat with the young lay-assistant at St Augustine's, Tim Hayes, and we quickly became great friends.

The church building had huge problems, and Robin, together with the church council, came up with ambitious plans to demolish all but a couple of pillars and build a brand new modern church. It was to be in the heart of the community: 'a church without walls', with glass sides around the main worship space so that passers-by could see straight in. It was to have a café, a local library, and a completely different feel from a traditional parish church. One Sunday we symbolically marched out of the old church, led by the cross and the robed choir, to our temporary home in an old mission hall 400 metres away. Two years of hard work in fund-raising and prayer followed, including a madcap sponsored trip where four of us climbed the highest peaks in Scotland, England and Wales in twenty-four hours while wearing choir surplices! Finally, in 1986, we moved back into the brand new St Augustine's. Those who marched back up the hill to the new church were nearly twice as many as those who'd left, as the time of transition had become a time of great growth in numbers and in faith for all who were involved.

At the same time as enjoying work and church in Bradford, another very significant development was taking place elsewhere in my life. In the summer of 1985, Tim Hayes persuaded me to help out with a beach mission at Dawlish Warren in South Devon. He'd asked me to lead the children's work, which involved organizing bizarre beach games and competitions for holidaymakers, and using drama, music and humour to tell Bible stories. My team was mainly made up of students and sixth formers, and soon one particular young lady, Anne Simons, with her blue eyes, and brown hair streaked with blonde highlights, began to catch my notice.

Saturday, 10 August 1985 was the only day off in the middle of the fortnight's mission. I had gradually been getting to know Anne over the previous week and increasingly liked what I saw and heard. I was shocked to discover that she was only seventeen and still studying for A levels. I was by now twenty-three and teaching, but she seemed to have a calm maturity as well as a wicked sense of fun, and I found her irresistible. I was keen to spend the day off with her, and suggested that we spend it walking on nearby Dartmoor. Anne asked if I could also invite her two tent-mates, Sharon and Louise, as they had no transport and nothing arranged for that day. I had really hoped to spend time alone with Anne, but realized I was dealing with somebody who consistently puts other people before herself, so, slightly crestfallen, I agreed and also invited my tent-mate, Roy, to come along.

Five people in one tiny orange Mini was always ambitious, especially when you added a guitar and various other bits and pieces, but the car coped well . . . at least to begin with. We had a good day, climbing Mam Tor and singing at the top, with nobody else in view, enjoying a pub lunch, seeing how close we could get to Dartmoor Prison without being arrested – but I didn't manage to get any time alone with Anne. Finally, as we drove back towards Dawlish Warren, the little Mini spluttered, choked and then stopped completely. The car wouldn't respond to anything, and we were miles from anywhere, in an era before mobile phones, and only dressed for a summer's day out. We reckoned we were about fifteen miles from Dawlish Warren and that we still had about five hours of daylight left. So we walked, hoping we would find some help along the way. To begin with, it was an adventure and we sang and joked as we went. After passing through a village where the police station was closed (our only chance of letting our friends know what had happened), we finally realized we were on our own and faced with a long trek ahead.

With unsuitable footwear – including flip-flops – and various levels of fitness, we became increasingly tired and footsore. Gradually the group spread out, Anne and I walking at the rear, at last giving us a chance to talk one-to-one. Looking back, both of us remember only a few details from that long afternoon and evening – sore feet, beautiful, clear, star-filled skies as darkness fell, and finding more and more in common as we shared our hopes and histories. We both had vicars for dads, both felt a strong call to cross-cultural mission, and we even (embarrassing as it is now to recollect) discussed how many children we dreamed of having! As the shooting stars lit the sky and reflected off the sea during the last few miles of seafront, our hands found each other and we drifted yet further behind the others.

The rest of the beach mission is a blur. Our friends had been increasingly worried about our absence, and were holding a prayer meeting for our welfare when we all arrived safely back. During the next week Anne and I shared precious moments in the late evenings, grabbing banana fritters and riding dodgem cars on the seafront funfair, but all too soon the fortnight was over. I travelled back to visit my parents and got ready for the new term in Bradford, as Anne returned to her parents' home near Bristol. Although I'd previously had a number of girlfriends, I knew I had found somebody very special and was desperate to see Anne again soon. As the letters started arriving, it was clear the feelings were mutual, but I was very aware of how the gap in miles and years would give us many challenges. A couple of weeks after Dawlish Warren, I (unusually) found myself attempting poetry:

Separation

It seems so long . . .
since pen kissed paper in a poem,
or thoughts were caught and crystallised in words.
I chase the butterflies of dreams
and pin them to a page,
and find mere words,
grey words.

It seems so long
since eye met eye in treasured glance
or prayers were shared beneath the shooting stars.
I search for metaphors of love,
but even rainbows fade,
and so do words,
pale words.

It seems so long
until . . . but why should we be sad?
For growth is slow in plants that would bear fruit.
We cry 'Impossible!' to God,
but mustard seeds make trees,
and even words
are seeds.
© Dave Bookless, 1985

Telling my Cambridge and Bradford friends that I had a new seventeen-year-old girlfriend led to some predictable ribbing, although once people had actually met Anne, it was amazing how quickly that stopped. More nerve-racking was the prospect of meeting her parents. Soon after term restarted I went down to Nailsea, a commuter town just south of Bristol, for the weekend. To their huge credit, Anne's parents, John and Jenny, made me feel completely at home and seemed totally unfazed by the age gap.

The next three years sped by, with lots of exhausting weekends, driving or catching trains between Bradford and Nailsea. My orange Mini finally went to the great junkyard in the sky, and was eventually replaced by an equally battered Fiat 127.

Meanwhile Anne and I expected that we would have a very long wait before the possibility of marriage. Long-distance relationships are never easy, but Anne needed to complete her A levels, carry out her plans to visit Thailand afterwards, and go on to study at university. Nevertheless we grew closer and closer, sharing our deepest thoughts and longings.

We both had a dream of cross-cultural Christian work in Asia, but somewhat different ideas of exactly where that should be. My heart was in India, while Anne had read many biographies of mission amongst the tribal groups who originated in China and are now spread through Laos, Cambodia and Thailand. She was even considering studying Chinese as part of her university course, and arranged to visit a Karen tribal village in Thailand for some months after A levels. While we grew closer emotionally, this became the one tension in our relationship. Eventually we reached the agonizing point where we jointly decided, against every-thing our hearts were screaming at us, that we should split up, as God seemed to be calling us to different parts of the world.

The next few weeks were among the lowest of my life. We broke off all direct contact. I found myself angry with God for bringing Anne into my life, and angry with myself for having allowed myself to fall so deeply in love with 'the wrong person'. I remember attending a service where, to the surprise and concern of my friends, I spent most of the time sobbing uncontrollably. At the end, the minister invited people to stay behind for prayer ministry, and said he particularly believed God wanted to heal the broken-hearted. I went forward, expecting words of comfort and reassurance, of God moving me on and helping me to get over Anne. Instead I heard something different. 'We believe God brought you together,' I was told, 'and he will lead you on together. Your call is to follow him as a couple – and let him sort out later where he wants you to serve him.'

My initial reaction was denial: I didn't want to be hurt so deeply again. What if I contacted Anne and she still felt God was calling us in different directions? Nervously I phoned and discovered she'd been waiting for me to call. Several wise, older friends had said exactly the same to her: that God was clearly calling us together, and he would guide us as to where – perhaps it would be to India and East Asia at different times, or perhaps even neither. From that moment it was only a matter of time. We got engaged in November 1986, and made plans to get married in the summer of 1988.

Looking back, both of us feel that our brief separation, agonizing as it was at the time, was vital. Without it, both of us would have spent the rest of our lives wrestling with whether we'd made the right decision. It was a time of giving up the most important relationship in our lives to God, of saying 'You come first, and I will give even this up for you if you want.' It felt a bit like God's challenge to Abraham to sacrifice his only son, Isaac (Genesis 22). He needed to be prepared to lose all that was most precious to him, before God pulled back and provided a ram instead. God sometimes tests us, not to taunt or torture us, but to strengthen our commitment to him and to toughen our resolve for hard times ahead. In all the trials that lay ahead, Anne and I would be able to look back and say with confidence that we had put God first and he had given us each other. For me it was also the start of learning that with God even the most painful and, at the time, meaningless experiences can eventually be redeemed into his loving purposes. With God, nothing need be wasted.

4 Cracking up

Living with people with disabilities has helped me to see my disabilities and to accept myself.[1]
Jean Vanier, founder of the L'Arche Communities

In the summer of 1986, just before A Levels, Anne caught a glandular fever-type virus, which knocked her out for several weeks. Although she recovered enough to sit most of her exams, her memory and concentration were affected, and her results weren't as predicted. The doctors gave her the all-clear to go to Thailand, where she was due to work alongside Gill Cockfield, a well-established missionary based in a remote Karen tribal village known as 'Prosperity Fields', near the Burmese border. The conditions were basic: wooden huts on stilts, no electricity or running water, cooking over open fires, but Anne was in her element and loved getting to know the village children and their parents, communicating with smiles and mime more than with words. However, after some weeks her energy levels began to dissipate, exhaustion overwhelmed her, and she realized that something was very badly wrong with her health. Her final weeks in Thailand were spent trying to discover the cause.

Returning to England, Anne was a ghostly version of the healthy young woman of a few months previously.

Fearing an obscure tropical disease, she was referred to Ham Green Hospital outside Bristol. Test after test again proved negative, until one specialist suggested a completely different diagnosis. Hearing about her earlier glandular fever, he suggested she was suffering from something called postviral fatigue syndrome. Later this became a definite diagnosis of what is also known as myalgic encephalo-myelitis (ME) or chronic fatigue syndrome. We had never heard of ME at the time. All we knew was that Anne was physically very weak and pallid, with severe joint pain, swollen glands, and energy levels that varied hugely from day to day. Her diet was also affected, with food intolerances to wheat and gluten.

When somebody close becomes ill with virus-type symp-toms, most people assume it will only be a few days, or at worst weeks, before they will be back to normal. Little did we know then that it would be eight long years before Anne would have her health back. We read all we could about ME/CFS and discovered that it was still somewhat contro-versial medically. The fact that the diagnosis was based on ruling everything else out, and by clusters of symptoms and the length of time they persisted, rather than by a simple blood test, meant that some more cautious doctors were unconvinced. The trigger often seemed to be a virus such as glandular fever, with longer-term effects caused when the body's immune system failed to react effectively to the initial virus. It was often otherwise fit and healthy young adults, like Anne, who were particularly prone, although people of all ages could be affected.

In Anne's case the symptoms were towards the severe end of the spectrum. She was confined to bed most of the time, with chronic pain in her joints, swollen glands, and often unable even to focus her mind enough to read a book. Perhaps not surprisingly, and particularly after news that her mother was suffering from an inoperable and life-threatening bowel cancer, Anne began to slide into a deep depression, questioning why God was allowing all this to happen.

As her boyfriend, then fiancé, and eventually husband, I found all of this extremely difficult. By nature I was not someone to take such medical conditions seriously. To be honest, if I hadn't known how healthy Anne was, witnessed her joy in living and heard her plans for the future, I would probably have been among those thinking her ME was 'all in the mind'. Instead, I could see how frustrated she was, how genuinely physical the pain was, and I felt totally unable to help. But when she began to be depressed, I again failed to understand. Surely we had so much to look forward to together? How could she be in love with me and yet feel her life wasn't worth living? Why, I argued simplistically, couldn't she realize God was still there despite her circumstances, pull herself together, and get on with life?

With Anne's patient help and explanation, I slowly began to understand more, both about ME and about depression. Although I may have felt useless, it seemed that just being there, listening to her and holding her, helped a bit. She was having prayer counselling with two women in her church, and was given Psalm 139 as 'homework', taking a verse that particularly spoke to her and repeating it until it had sunk into her subconscious, or painting her response to it. Written three thousand years ago, this psalm speaks of how each person is known individually by God from before the moment of conception, and is divinely shaped and cared for. It speaks of God's presence with us, wherever we travel, whatever situations overwhelm us, whether or not we feel God is there. For Anne, Psalm 139, and the scrapbook she created of paintings, calligraphy and photographs based upon it, became a very tangible and effective part of her healing from the depths of depression. Alongside the help from anti-depressants, and the love and care of those of us who were closest to her, God's words of love caused her slowly to recover a sense of worth and identity in the midst of her ME.

We were married in July 1988, at Holy Trinity, Nailsea, where Anne's father was vicar. The service was a wonderful celebration of God's faithfulness and of human love. Robin Gamble from Bradford preached a slightly risqué sermon, Tim Hayes as best man told some juicy anecdotes in his speech, and a wide group of family and friends provided the food for the reception. Anne had rested for weeks beforehand to build up her strength, and was able to walk down the aisle and stand beside me for the ceremony, before sitting for the rest of the service.

I had left my work in Bradford shortly before our wedding, so we had the luxury of nearly a month's honeymoon, exploring the most northerly part of Britain, the Shetland Isles with their rocky coastline, stunning views and wonderful wildlife. Anne's ME was in slight remission and she was able to enjoy short walks. We spent hours sitting on clifftops, laughing at the comic waddling and squawking of puffins, creeping over rocks to catch a glimpse of otters, and enjoying freshly caught fish in front of peat fires.

Amazingly, Anne also appeared to have been healed from her gluten allergy. Some friends had specifically prayed about this before the wedding, hoping she'd be able to enjoy the wedding cake. However, we'd not wanted to risk spoiling the big day with Anne getting ill, so our friend, Christine Higginson, who made the cake, also specially made a tiny gluten-free one for Anne. When we got to the Shetlands though, staying largely in small bed and breakfast accommodation, food choices were fairly limited and hunger drove Anne to eat bread – but with no ill effects. It remains a mystery to us why God relieved her of the gluten allergy but did not take away the ME at the same time, yet prayer is always a bit like that. God always answers, but all too rarely at exactly the moment or precisely in the way we want or hope. We have to trust that he sees the big picture, even when we cannot see it.

The reason why I had resigned from my work in Bradford was that I had recently been accepted for ordination in the Church of England. The 'call' was not a dramatic one, but rather a series of gradual nudges: encouraging comments when I'd led worship or preached at St Augustine's, the experience of leading teams on missions such as at Dawlish Warren, and several of the people I most respected suggesting I should explore the possibility of getting ordained. Robin Gamble was inspirational, and John Simons also patiently encouraged me. My own parents were delighted too, although they never pushed me towards ordination. The process of interviews and selection panels was a bit arcane and tedious at times, yet I trusted that through this God would work either in shutting the door, or in opening it to allow me into a new sphere of Christian ministry. Anne, after getting over her initial hang-ups from having grown up in the goldfish bowl of a vicarage, also encouraged me to pursue ordination.

So, when we returned from the Shetland Isles, it was neither to live in Bradford nor Nailsea, but to create a new married home in a little one-bedroom flat belonging to Trinity Theological College, Bristol. Both of us signed up for a three-year degree course in theology. In Anne's case, ill health had prevented her from going to university beforehand, and she had enjoyed studying A Level RE while ill, so we had the rare privilege of beginning married life as students together.

Studying theology at Trinity proved to be an immensely rich and stretching experience. I was far more focused and motivated than I had been as an undergraduate, and loved wrestling with gritty ethical dilemmas, learning how to preach more effectively, and thinking through issues of theology and philosophy. Anne and I also made great friends among the students and staff, as well as in placement churches.

There was now the chance to think theologically about many of the encounters with other faiths I had experienced in Bradford. In fact one of the reasons why I had chosen Trinity was the presence on the staff of Colin Chapman, a widely experienced leader in the field of Christian–Muslim relations. Eventually, with Colin's encouragement, came an opportunity to write a Grove booklet, *Interfaith Worship and Christian Truth*, which would be published in 1991 just as we left Bristol.

I was also able to spend my final year doing a masters degree on 'Church, Religion and Society 1780–1940', combining my theological and historical background. For the main dissertation I looked at the influence of an Indian Christian figure who had always fascinated me, Sadhu Sundar Singh, who lived from 1889 to 1929.

Born into a Sikh family that valued Islam and Hinduism but saw Christianity as a Western religion, Sundar Singh entered a deep suicidal despair after the death of his mother. He then had a vision of an Urdu-speaking, Indian-dressed Jesus, which led to his conversion, and he spent the rest of his short life travelling through India, preaching and teaching in a style that combined the traditional Hindu sadhu, or holy man, with the parable stories beloved by Jesus. In his day he was nationally and internationally famous, attracting enormous crowds from all faith backgrounds wherever he travelled, in India and beyond. Yet his one visit to the UK, like his contemporary Gandhi's, convinced him that the 'Christian West' had sold out. He likened Western Christians to a stone in a stream: so hardened by their love for material possessions that the life-giving water of the gospel was unable to penetrate through the outer shell of their materialistic lives. He himself wore the simplest of clothes, and his only possessions were a few books. He finally lost his life when he disappeared while trying to walk across the Himalayas to take the message of his Guru Jesus to Tibet. Today he is still remembered and revered by Christians and others in India.

My dissertation looked at 'The water of life in an Indian cup', the way in which his lifestyle so attractively combined the message of Jesus with Indian culture. I was able to spend time researching in the archives of mission agencies stored in the School of Oriental and African Studies in London, where I found dozens of previously unstudied letters from the sadhu to his contemporaries. Sadhu Sundar Singh, both for his teaching and even more for his lifestyle, has remained an enduring influence on my life ever since this period, and his critique of Western Christianity has continued to shape my own thinking.

It was while I was at Trinity that the events which begin this book also took place: the holiday on the Isles of Scilly, throwing away our rubbish, and God's unexpected voice. It forced me to ask why, in a life of attending churches, reading Christian books, and now studying theology, I had received virtually no teaching at all about the environment. You might think that a Bible college would be a good place to grapple with the Bible, and mostly you'd be right. However, as l looked through the syllabus for material on caring for creation, I looked in vain. There were courses on preaching and pastoral care, on mission and ministry, on doctrine and discipleship, but nothing on relating to the world in which we live. 'Creation' was only mentioned in two places: in a lecture series on the Old Testament book of Job (of which more later), and in discussions about the origin of the universe: the old chestnut of 'creationism vs evolution'. This wasn't what I was looking for. It seemed to me then, and still does now, that God is far more interested in how we treat his amazing world, than in what we believe about how he made it.

Yet as I turned to the Bible itself, I was astonished at how, again and again, the whole creation (not just human beings) is at the heart of God's purposes. Familiar passages I thought I knew came alive as I reread them, asking, 'What does this say about how God sees the non-human creation?' The very first chapters of the Bible, where God creates human beings from the dust of the earth and places them in a garden to look after and care for it, struck me forcibly. Looking after the earth and its creatures is foundational to what it means to be human – it is the very first great commission in Scripture. Looking further on, the account of Noah and the ark challenged my ideas on God's priorities: very few human beings get rescued, but God seems particularly concerned about biodiversity conservation, ensuring that breeding stocks of every living species are protected. After the ark eventually rested on dry land, God's covenant, his ever-lasting promise never again to destroy the earth, is not just with human beings, but with every living creature, and even with the earth itself.

Jumping ahead to the New Testament, Jesus' arrival is marked by angels promising 'peace on earth', not simply an end to war, but God's peace, a 'shalom' harmony that extends to animals and ecosystems. The reason God sent Jesus is because 'God so loved the world' (John 3:16) – the word is *kosmos* in the original Greek, a word that usually conveyed then what it does now. He died and rose not just to rescue individual human beings, but so that all things in heaven and earth might be reconciled to God (Colossians 1:19–20). New, often shocking, discoveries kept tumbling out of the pages of the Bible, and I was astonished at how I had missed them for so many years.

This was radical stuff that shifted my world-view. I realized that I had been deeply unbiblical in assuming that God's purpose in making this amazing world had been focused only on human beings. He made this world not for us, but for himself: all things are made for Christ (Colossians 1:16). Other species are not merely extras in a play that's all about people – they matter to God in and for themselves. There is no hint in the story of Noah that God saved all the other creatures for Noah's benefit. Rather they were to be rescued 'so they [could] multiply on the earth and be fruitful and increase in number upon it' (Genesis 8:17) – in other words they had intrinsic value to God.

Alongside the excitement of discovering new truths, and the mental stimulation of theological college, Anne and I were facing bigger challenges in our own lives. Surveys say that getting married, moving house and changing job are among the most stressful experiences people go through, and we had just gone through all three at once. Perhaps it's not surprising that Anne's fragile health began to decline again, as she suffered a relapse of her ME. The agonizing pain of her joints, and the need to rest her body, made it very hard to concentrate on lectures. Trinity College kindly provided her with a bedsit in college, and using a system of baby monitors she was able to listen to lectures lying down, while I took notes that we could both use later. She worked incredibly hard, and in our three years eventually managed to complete two years of course work and assessments, earning herself a Dip HE in theology.

However, as if the ME wasn't bad enough, when we tried to start a family Anne suffered repeated miscarriages. The first one hit us both hard. We were so excited about having a child, and it seemed grossly unfair that this tiny life should be snatched away. It affected Anne in a deeper way than I could really understand, profoundly shaking her faith in God's goodness. We followed lots of good advice about grieving, giving each baby a name, and talking about them together, but that didn't make it any easier. Like the ME, this carried on beyond college, and eventually we had five consecutive miscarriages, the last one, Charlotte, after nearly five months of pregnancy. We gave her a full funeral, and still visit her grave at Mortlake cemetery each year.

Taken together, Anne's ME and the miscarriages gave us many struggles with God. I came to realize that it was all very well for me to talk about a good and loving God when my experience of life had been so comfortable and protected. Now I was being exposed, not just to Anne's suffering and our loss, but to the tip of a huge and frightening iceberg of the whole world's pain, which threatened to smash and sink the frail vessel of my faith. I became more aware of people I knew with depression, disabilities, injustices and heartaches. I watched the TV news with its pictures of disaster victims, and felt differently from before. Something inside me identified with the pain of others in a way I hadn't known. Everywhere I turned there was terrifying suffering.

I remember going for a walk on my own in Leigh Woods on the edge of Bristol, arguing with God. 'Where are you?' I cried aloud in my anger and pain. The line of an old prayer of John Donne came into my mind: 'Batter my heart, three-personed God'. And I wanted to batter at God's heart, to get answers to my questions. But they never came. At least not in the ways I wanted or expected them to come. At last, like a ranting toddler running out of energy, I felt exhausted and became quiet. I sat down at the base of a big old oak tree and I wept. Slowly I became aware of my surroundings: of the trees and their branches moving gently in the breeze, of the yellow and orange autumn leaves carpeting the ground, slowly and silently rotting down. I heard no voice, but a subtle rewiring started to take place within my mind. I felt the solid trunk of the tree, which had survived so many storms, and then saw how flexible its branches were, responding to each whisper of breeze. I began to question my own search for neat simple answers. Maybe I needed to be like the tree, and to allow my faith to combine deep roots with a flexible openness. After all, the tree that stops growing stops living.

I also looked at the leaves and thought of their short lives, decorating the tree for a season and then falling, dying, rotting, turning into fertile mulch, and through that putting goodness back into the soil. Was this what Jesus meant when he told us to 'look at the flowers of the field'? We are all fragile. Life is brief but precious. Death is a necessary part of the natural cycle. Nothing is wasted – God doesn't do waste. It is only our comfortable, insulated Western societies that get surprised by suffering, illness and death. In places where people are more connected to the rhythms of nature and the cycles of the seasons, perhaps they are better prepared to understand pain and loss.

When I got back to college, I listened more closely to a lecture series from John Bimson on the Old Testament book of Job: a book that spends forty-two chapters wrestling with the problem of a good God and random evil. Job begins as a man who has everything – wealth, health, family, respect, reputation, and a devout faith in God. All of this is stripped away and he is left with nothing, nothing at all. Even his friends desert him, accusing him of having brought disaster on himself by upsetting God. After many chapters in which his friends give every conventional answer about suffering, Job is taken out into the desert, and there, amid weird creatures and wild landscapes, he encounters God again. To my surprise I discovered that Job had found answers to his questions not in wisdom, reasoned argument or even religion, but in God speaking to him through nature. 'Look at the ostrich,' says God. 'Isn't it stupid? Do you understand it? Well then, how can you hope to understand the one who made it?' 'Who looks after the places where no human being has ever been?' God asks. 'Who made the weird creatures of the earth, the hippopotamus and the crocodile? Do you understand them? Can you control them? Perhaps,' says God, 'I am at work in ways that are beyond your imagination, that you can't begin to understand.'

Like Job I found that looking at the natural world began to change my perspective on suffering: creation's vastness and beauty, its rhythms and patterns, and yet also the suffering and rawness of nature. My experience wasn't unique, for suffering is a natural part of the human condition in a groaning creation. And there is not always an obvious purpose or pattern in the suffering either. Yet there is, behind it and within it, the hand of an awesome, creative and loving God, who can transform even the most terrible suffering into something worthwhile and life-giving.

As well as discovering Job, I found that I was relating to the death and resurrection of Jesus in a completely new way. Here was God, not as a distant, remote, unfeeling dictator, allowing his subjects to suffer. Here instead was a God who got his hands dirty, who chose to take on the limitations of humanity, knowing that unbelievable pain and suffering were to be his destiny. There are hints of this in the Old Testament, but it is only in Jesus that we see it worked out fully. Jesus experienced terrible suffering, and therefore I could go to God with my own questions, pain and anger. God in Jesus also showed that suffering does not have to be the end. The resurrection of Jesus is not a fairy story: 'So they all lived happily ever after.' Instead it is the Creator himself dealing with what has gone wrong within creation, transforming and redeeming it through his own suffering, death and resurrection.

My most important learning experience at theological college was not what I absorbed in lectures, but in having my faith painfully shattered, reshaped and eventually restored. One day I woke early, trying to prepare some devotions for my college small group, and a prose poem bubbled up from somewhere deep inside. At the time, and since, other people seem to have found it helpful, perhaps because so many of us go through something of a spiritual crisis where our old views of the world shatter.

Cracks

There are cracks in my world.
I noticed them one day and now they are everywhere:
Sinister hairline cracks that start and finish out of sight,
cracks that grow and gape and laugh at my certainties.
My world has been declared unsafe.

I have tried to paper them over,
paint them out,
move the furniture to hide them,
but they always return,
cracks that hang like question marks in my mind.

And now I begin to think:
Why do the cracks appear?
From where do they come?
They have made my room unsafe
BUT

They have thrown it open to new horizons,
drawn back curtains,
raised long-closed shutters.
One day I looked and a crack had become a window.
Step through, it said, what have you to fear?
Do you wish to stay in your crumbling room?

And then I remembered a childhood dream,
watching the egg of some exotic bird,
oval and perfect, spotted blue and cream.
I wished to hold that egg and keep it on a shelf
BUT

As I watched it cracks appeared.
Tiny fissures spread like zigzag ripples.
It broke in two and life struggled to its feet,
wet and weak and blinking at the world.
Without those cracks that egg could hold
no more than rotting stagnant death.

Without its cracks my world would be
a room without a view.
Cracks may be uncomfortable, disturbing gaps
BUT

Could it be I need them?
Do you believe in cracks?
Because I keep looking for God in the room
and find he is hiding in the cracks.
© Dave Bookless, 1990

5 Riding the roller coaster

Most of the growth that's ever occurred in my life has occurred in the midst of great pain.[1]
John Wimber

When we left Bristol in 1991, it was for me to be ordained as a curate, apprenticed to St John's Church in Southall, West London. We expected to be in Southall for three or four years before moving elsewhere, possibly back to Bradford. We'd deliberately chosen to be in one of the most urban, multi-cultural corners of the UK, not just because of my Indian roots, but out of a strong sense that this was where God was leading us.

I had, as I've said before, always been puzzled that so many of my fellow theological students had set their hearts on large suburban churches, ministering to affluent, middle-class and often mono-cultural congregations. In the Bible, God has a clear heart for the outcast, the rejected, the poor and the 'foreigner'. I have a feeling that, were Jesus around today, he would choose to spend most of his time alongside those struggling in urban housing estates, among asylum seekers and refugees, or perhaps in economically deprived rural communities, rather than behind the gates and gardens of suburbia.

We had heard about St John's Southall from another student, and knew that it embraced a cross-section of cultures and nationalities: Indian, African, Caribbean, European and more. We had also met David Bronnert, the vicar, who had many years experience of cross-cultural ministry. St John's fitted the vision of church that Anne and I shared, not of a cold building containing a bunch of formal Europeans speaking seventeenth-century English, but a vibrant worshipping crowd of people from every nation, culture and language under the sun. This is a deeply biblical vision: the good news of Jesus breaking down the suspicions and hostilities between cultures and races (Galatians 3:28), and bringing people together in unity to worship Jesus (Revelation 7:9).

I quickly got stuck into parish life: preaching, funerals, youth club, confirmation classes, church councils and visiting the housebound. Preaching at St John's gave me an opportunity to explore things I had been learning while studying theology, including the struggles with suffering and healing that Anne's ME and the repeated miscarriages had provoked. I was also able to lead a series of studies on the relevance of Sadhu Sundar Singh to Christians today – and where better to do that than Southall with its largely Asian population?

Life as a curate was busy and fulfilling, yet we still had a sense of being prepared for something else. The environmental questions that had started on the Isles of Scilly wouldn't go away, but rather niggled like a persistent toothache. I remember nervously preaching for the first time on the environment, focusing on how God is an expert in recycling. He takes broken messed-up people and recycles them into new creations in Christ; he also takes all the rotting leaves and fallen trees, and the remains of dead animals, and remakes them into new things. I suggested that we should be more careful of our wastefulness, because with God nothing ever gets wasted. Afterwards various people came to speak to me, having been provoked or challenged. Like me they had never had any teaching on this subject before.

By this time I was looking around for other Christians who were concerned about caring for creation. I wanted a group who were both biblically based and practically involved, doing something hands-on, expressing the Genesis call to care for God's world in a tangible way.

Eventually, early in 1993, I came across an article in a Christian magazine about some anniversary celebrations for a Christian nature conservation group called A Rocha. Apparently there had been a Christian-based field studies and environmental education centre on the Algarve coast in Portugal for ten years, and, better still, they were having a gathering in London to celebrate. The speaker was the Revd Dr John Stott, the highly respected author and Bible teacher. Everybody was welcome, so along I went.

This event was a major turning point. John Stott's talk on Psalm 19, 'The Word of God and the works of God', described, in a way I found very helpful, how God speaks to us, both through the Bible and through creation. I was equally impressed by the A Rocha people I met: Peter and Miranda Harris, who had lived in Portugal for ten years getting A Rocha going, and talked with honesty, humility and enthusiasm about the joys and stresses of protecting the environment, living in community, and working to get across the message of God's love for all creation. By the end of the meeting I wanted to know more. I went home and asked Anne if she fancied a holiday the following year, volunteering with A Rocha in Portugal.

In the end we went twice in 1994, using up most of our holiday allowance, to volunteer at Cruzinha, A Rocha's Portuguese centre. These were wonderful breaks, away from urban Southall, swapping the cold, dirty streets of London for a Mediterranean climate with sunshine, blue seas, good food and great people. I spent time counting wading birds, helping with meals and washing up, learning to catch and ring birds to study their migration, and enjoying lots of long conversations with A Rocha team members. Meanwhile Anne's ME was really bad, and she was too ill to do very much more than soak up the sunshine, or lie in bed while Miranda Harris came and read stories to her. Occasionally I would push Anne around in her wheelchair. This proved to be a somewhat dangerous experience for her because, when birdwatchers see something rare or interesting, they tend to let go of everything else and grab their binoculars. Thankfully Anne forgave me for any unexpected bruises she gained on the dusty tracks around Cruzinha.

But what really affected us deeply about what we saw modelled in Portugal was the way in which it brought together so many threads that had already become important to us. Here were Christians simply living out their faith in a full and honest way in the real world. Visitors and volunteers were, and still are, welcomed, whether or not they considered themselves Christians. In caring for wildlife the team didn't stop caring for people – in fact we'd rarely met such unconditional love. There was a true sense of community: not the closed community of a clique, but an open-ended invitation to anybody to join in. What we saw at Cruzinha was the Christian gospel lived out in a full and holistic way: good news for people but also for the whole creation; good news in word but also in action. By now we were hooked, and discussed there and then whether God might want us to be some part of A Rocha in the future.

There were only two problems. First, Anne was seriously ill, and secondly we believed God had called us to urban ministry in London. By late 1993 I had moved from St John's to help look after a neighbouring Southall church, St George's, and I was committed to staying there for at least five years.

Now St George's was not the kind of church I had ever imagined I would end up at. Unlike St John's, where the worship was contemporary and uncluttered, St George's had a very strong Anglo-Catholic tradition. This meant that I had to learn things I'd never been taught at theological college: which coloured vestments to wear in what seasons and how to swing the thurible with incense. I struggled with some traditions but made a deal with the church council: if they could give me good biblical or pastoral reasons why we should continue something, I would happily do it, but otherwise they would have to be prepared for changes.

However, while it wasn't my tradition, there was much that I gradually came to appreciate in the worship at St George's. The use of symbolism and the senses – colours to indicate the changing seasons, the smell of incense to bring an awareness of God's holy presence – were all helpful in a multicultural congregation where many did not speak English as their first language. Similarly, liturgy meant people could learn the prayers by heart, enabling them to join in if they were illiterate or spoke poor English.

Coming to St George's, I had also inherited a whole series of other challenges: a major legal case hovering over the church hall; a small and sometimes divided congregation; a church building that had been used regularly by other faith groups; a vast vicarage that in places hadn't been properly cleaned for decades.

But worst of all, Anne's fifth pregnancy had just ended prematurely. Baby Charlotte, mentioned earlier, had died at birth, with multiple abnormalities, in the fifth month of pregnancy. While Anne and I were physically and emotionally devastated and full of questions about our unanswered prayers, we decided to be completely open with people about what we were going through.

Slowly things at St George's changed. The small congregation, largely Punjabi Indian and Grenadian Caribbean, responded well to a few modern songs introduced on the guitar, to preaching that was simple and well illustrated, and to the introduction of prayer ministry during the communion service. A few more people started coming, some who had previously attended but had been frightened away by a sad recent history of arguments and bitterness, others from Sikh, Hindu and Muslim backgrounds who found a welcome and a sense of God's presence there. Bit by bit, through prayer and through patiently nurturing relationships, many of the other problems surrounding the church faded away. The legal case was dropped and the hall returned to the church, freeing up space for children's and youth work and community projects. Groups from other faiths realized that St George's was no longer about to close as a place of Christian worship, and began to look elsewhere for places to meet.

There isn't space here to tell in detail the story of change and transformation at St George's. We had some intensely painful episodes, with people leaving as they saw changes they could not cope with, and other deeply scarred individuals staying on but hurting those around them. There were also hilarious moments, from the occasion when the verger emptied the red-hot charcoal from the thurible into a bin full of paper, causing rather more smoke than usual as the vestry nearly caught fire, through to the occasion when the visiting bishop was interrupted during his sermon by a lady asking where to find the toilet.

There was the slightly scary moment when we discovered that the 'Somali fashion show' that had booked the church hall was actually a front for a banned Islamic extremist group, and when I returned from a day off to find massed ranks of police blocking the road with a helicopter hovering over the vicarage.

Then there was the joy of working with others: Sue Jelfs who came to join us as a community outreach worker (we only realized what the initials spelt after we'd appointed her!), spending long hours befriending people from many faith backgrounds and sharing Jesus' love with them, and a series of young volunteer Careforce workers from abroad: Letlal from India, Kiki from Kenya, Shirley from Bolivia, and Kuki from India who shared our home for two years and became not only godmother to one of our children, but a close friend and adopted sister to Anne and myself.

There were also many, many deeply moving moments, sharing people's joys and sorrows: the amazing Asian wedding celebrations and the powerful Caribbean funerals when the church sometimes had nearly 1,000 people crammed in. Best of all there was the huge privilege of seeing the tender shoots of faith take root and grow in people's lives: the person who had been coming for forty years who, after an Alpha course, finally understood the gospel for himself; the tough lorry driver, wrongly imprisoned after somebody had hidden drugs in his vehicle, who shared how the songs and Bible verses he'd learned since coming to St George's had stopped him losing his mind in prison; the teenager I'd seen grow from childhood into faith who gave her first talk in church and brought me to the edge of tears. When we would eventually move on after seven years, the congregation would have almost tripled in size, many people would have come to faith or grown in their Christian faith, and the church would be unrecognizable.

But one of the most powerful things we learned from our time at St George's was right at the beginning. With Anne confined to bed and helpless, and me spending much of my time nursing her and doing the necessary shopping, cooking and cleaning, I arrived not as a 'great white hope' (with all the connotations those words contain) but tired and vulnerable, not as a do-it-all vicar but as a deeply human being. In a church full of hurting people, many who had never been allowed to think that God could employ them, God used our weakness to show the topsy-turvy strength of his kingdom. People discovered that, rather than needing a vicar to lead their church, the vicar needed them, and many rallied round in very practical ways, dropping off food, and helping to clean and redecorate the big old vicarage. Our weakness made space for God to act and for others to discover their gifts.

* * *

What happened with Anne's illness is worth telling in more detail, not only because it was extraordinary, but because, without it, we could never have moved on to what lay ahead. When we returned from our first visit to Portugal in mid-1994, Anne was physically at her most disabled – confined to bed and wheelchair. Yet for the first time in eight years of illness she had reached a place of acceptance regarding her ME. We and others had prayed for her physical healing many times, with everything the Bible encouraged – anointing with oil, the laying on of hands, fasting, and more. Now Anne had reached a point of seeing that God might want her to remain disabled long term, perhaps even for ever, and she was able to accept that, if it was God's will. 'I'm yours,' she said. 'Whether ill or well, let me be what you want me to be.' I'd got used to caring for her and felt the same way. If God could use us better with Anne's ME, in our weakness, then we were willing to accept that.

But very soon after this a friend invited us to a special meeting at a nearby church, St Andrew's, Chorleywood. There was to be a guest speaker from America and prayer ministry available afterwards. I explained that, with Anne being so unwell, we didn't go to meetings, and that she'd reached a place of peace about her illness. But our friend persisted – the focus of the prayer ministry wasn't on healing, it was on 'more of God', opening ourselves up to allow God to give us more of his love, his power, his Spirit.

We relented, and I self-consciously pushed Anne into a full church, where the only space for her wheelchair was in the very front row, with, we felt, every eye looking at us. Neither of us can remember anything about the speaker but, when the invitation came for prayer, I suddenly realized how emotionally and spiritually exhausted I felt. All the effort of caring for Anne, of moving house and job, of the hard work and arguments surrounding the church, came flooding over me, and I stood with my hands palms upwards asking God to fill up my emptiness. There was a tremendous sense of anticipation all around the room, and I can remember just soaking in a deep sense of God's love. When I looked down at Anne, sitting in her chair, I saw that she was praying quietly, also receiving. Later she told me that she had seen a mental picture of the huge but gentle lion, Aslan, from C. S. Lewis's Narnia books, walking around the room, breathing on people to give them new life, sometimes gently placing a giant paw on someone's forehead, causing them to fall to the floor where they lay resting. Then one of the ministers from the church, Barry Kissell, whom we knew, came over and asked Anne if he could pray with her. Anne had an overwhelming sensation of God's love flowing right through her body from head to toe, and with amazement she realized that, after eight years of illness, she was being healed from her ME.

We waited until nearly everybody had left before Anne cautiously tried to stand up. She walked, right out of the church, pushing her wheelchair in front of her! At home her wasted leg muscles ached as she walked up the stairs, but there was no reaction and she could feel the strength slowly returning. A couple of days later there was a strange relapse, with the old ME aches in her glands and joints returning. Confused, we rang Barry and he offered to pray again. If God had started healing Anne, surely he did not want to turn the clock back? This time Anne felt absolutely nothing when she was prayed for, and yet since that day she has never had even the slightest relapse of her ME. She was well once again: fully back to the woman I'd fallen in love with nine years previously.

The next few weeks were a whirlwind. Anne went to her doctor to explain what had happened and to ask about cancelling her Severe Disablement Allowance and returning her disabled car-parking badge. The doctor was cautious, insisting that she wait some weeks, but eventually he had to admit he had no medical explanation for what had happened to her. Around Southall rumours spread like wildfire, and we had all sorts of people turning up at church, including Muslims, Sikhs and Hindus, all hoping to be healed of various awful conditions. We prayed for them all, and some experienced healing but by no means all. We explained to everybody that there was no magic in this, that the most important thing was not the healing but the Healer, Jesus, who could not only remove our illnesses, but also heal the broken heart, the troubled mind, the wounded soul, and deliver from sin.

We also received many invitations to speak at churches about Anne's healing. But for us this was deeply frustrating. It was our experience that God had been powerfully at work through Anne's illness and in our repeated miscarriages, yet we had had few requests to speak then. Only now that Anne had undergone 'a dramatic miracle healing' were churches interested in her story. Sadly it seemed to us that many churches were simply reflecting our 'instant gratification' culture, only wanting to hear stories about 'success' and about defeating pain and suffering. Yet the biblical stories we read were far more true to the downs as well as the ups of our experience – stories of God at work through suffering as well as through healing. In the end we only accepted invitations from churches where we were free to talk not only about how God works through healing, but about all that God can do through pain and suffering as well.

We were often asked how God could heal some people but not others. There are no easy answers to satisfy somebody struggling with long-term suffering, but in the end two key thoughts have helped us. One is to remind ourselves whom we're dealing with. God is not a slot machine: insert your prayer and out pops the answer you wanted. God is God! He is the Almighty Creator whose purposes are far beyond our understanding, who can sometimes allow things that we feel are terrible and unjust, because he sees the bigger picture. The second realization is that we live in a battle zone between good and evil. When Jesus walked this earth he healed the sick and showed that God's rule, God's kingdom, can break into this broken, spoiled world. When he rose from death, he defeated evil once and for all, yet until Jesus returns we are in the 'in-between times'. Suffering, evil and death therefore remain part of everybody's experience. We can also see signs of God's coming perfect, peaceful rule, when all sickness and suffering will be wiped away, whenever God heals the sick, mends broken relationships, changes despair to hope, and begins the restoration of a broken world.

* * *

Anne's dramatic healing took place late in the summer of 1994, and within weeks we found she was pregnant with Hannah Cruzinha, who was to be our first live child, born in June 1995, and would eventually be followed at roughly two-year intervals by three sisters, Rebekah, Bethany-Rose (better known as Rosie) and Naomi-Ruth. Meanwhile, our big vicarage at St George's became full, not only with babies and toddlers, but with a variety of people from around the world, as we tried to put into practice something of the model of community living we'd experienced at A Rocha Portugal. We learned to share our home, our food, our television choices, our jokes, and our good and bad moods with them all: with Kuki and later Letlal from India, Ron and Fazlin from

Malaysia, Glenn from Yorkshire, Sue who'd worked in India and France, and Colin who described himself as a 'world citizen'. Many others stayed with us for days or weeks, sometimes including some or even all of the six children of a single mum from our church who periodically needed a break.

Living in community is never an easy business, because people see you as you really are, and often hold up a mirror to your least attractive qualities. Not only do you soon get annoyed by the little things other people do, like leaving the toilet seat up or down (depending on your gender!), not putting away the washing up, or tramping through the house with muddy feet, you also soon learn that you're not as nice as you thought you were. You become aware of your own irritating habits, your irrational prejudices, your bad moods, and of how you've been shaped by hurts and bad relationships in your own past. Yet at the same time, living in community is also the most powerful witness to how God can transform broken people and can create 'the body of Christ' – a diverse group of people who together show Jesus.

One of the characteristics of modern life is that people are leading increasingly isolated lives. Many want their own space, their own home, their own private world. Some of this is necessary, for if you've spent a long day commuting to work crammed with hundreds of other people on the bus or train, and then all day having to 'perform' in front of work colleagues, you need to be able to crash out and enjoy some space. But perhaps the pendulum has swung too far. Today's tragic breakdown in family and community life is having a knock-on impact in terms of mental illness, broken relationships, and young people growing up without positive role models. If the old forms of community weren't working, that does not mean we should throw out the whole concept of 'community', but we need instead to find new spaces to belong to, and new groups to be accountable to, helping us to develop and grow as people.

In our attempts to share our lives with others, our family made lots of mistakes. We discovered that growing children do need some time and space with just their parents. For a while our children were quite genuinely confused as to who was part of their family and who simply shared the house. So we created the 'Bookless Bunch' – our own family identity – and made sure that certain rooms and special times were kept just for us. This proved to be increasingly important as the girls grew older. We, or should I say I, also discovered that people have different attitudes to arguing. I had always assumed that an old-fashioned shouting match was the best way to solve a disagreement. It didn't stop me loving other people, it was just how I dealt with things. It took me a long time to realize that others might see this as intimidating, or even frightening, and that I could really hurt people without meaning to. Community living is a great cure for pride, and my need for everything to be resolved was severely challenged when somebody simply cleared their room and walked out after an argument! There was bad feeling, they didn't contact us at all for several years, and we had no opportunity to tie up the loose ends. Today the relationship is healed and we've become friends again, but it took many years to repair the bridges.

As well as experimenting with community life, I was getting more involved with A Rocha. Although its only project was still in Portugal, there were supporters around the UK, and I was asked to speak on A Rocha's behalf. I was also invited to become a trustee of the charity and soon discovered that there were emerging ideas of 'other A Rochas' beyond Portugal, with possibilities in Lebanon and Kenya. We weren't the only ones who'd been inspired by Cruzinha and wished to see if something similar could happen elsewhere. I offered to explore possibilities for an A Rocha project in the UK, and received details of a variety of sites that A Rocha supporters felt were possibilities.

It was an enjoyable way to spend a day off – travelling to wild, beautiful coastal areas and dreaming of setting up an A Rocha centre – and I spent many days off doing just that. Together with the other trustees, I developed a list of key criteria for a project. It needed to be in an area that was important for wildlife, yet where we wouldn't be duplicating what other groups were already doing. It needed to be accessible by public transport. It needed to have a potential centre, a building with space for accommodation, offices, storage and community gathering. It needed to be fundable, for A Rocha had no savings of its own! Above all, it needed to have a sense of something special or 'magical' about it. I gradually worked my way around the country visiting the sites suggested by others, writing reports, but in each case the trustees sensed that, however wonderful they were, the sites didn't quite meet the criteria for A Rocha UK.

As I returned from these visits to the urban sprawl of Southall, I slowly realized that there was a wedge developing between our call to multicultural urban ministry and the pull we were now feeling towards A Rocha. It was going to be a very difficult choice as we could sense God at work in both. Was God calling me to stay as a vicar in an urban parish, or to set up an A Rocha centre? As usual my way of thinking things through, of trying to wrestle with a difficult problem, was to go for walks, away from people, to seek God's voice in the company of his creation.

Some time late in 1997, I first noticed a large area of empty space on the edge of Southall and decided to explore it. Technically it was part of St George's Parish, so I was simply doing my parish visiting! As I walked around I found somebody clearing up after a huge car boot sale. I discovered abandoned fridges and boxes of computer parts, plastic bags blown against the fence like a line of prayer flags, and thick muddy puddles spread everywhere by tyre marks. Walking on I found a pond full of reed mace, choked with rubbish, then a line of mature trees following an ancient field boundary. Following the tree line, avoiding the deep ruts from off-road motorbikes and burned-out cars, I reached a small river, which the map told me was Yeading Brook. Then I came to a bridge, which I crossed, and to a large metal fence with broken gates, so I walked on. I was now standing on a narrow strip of land between the river and the Grand Union Canal. It was totally overgrown with brambles, and with invasive introduced plants such as giant hogweed, Japanese knotweed and Himalayan balsam. Yet it was also a quiet place, where the distant hum of traffic from the M4 and the planes from Heathrow Airport faded into the background.

Standing there, I thanked God for this wild corner of west London that had somehow remained largely green. Hearing bird calls, I looked up with my binoculars. A flock of redpolls, small streaky finches with bright red foreheads, were flitting around in a birch tree by the canal. Then I heard a high-pitched call and glanced around as a kingfisher darted past, a flash of blue-green with an electric blue rump and a deep orange underside. Amazing! Here was a forgotten piece of deserted wilderness in the middle of urban sprawl. Here was a place that had suffered from neglect and deliberate abuse, yet still had traces of old meadows, hedges, trees and ponds with wildlife hanging on. As I walked home, I remembered those words God had whispered some years earlier, but this time they were slightly different: 'How do you think I feel about *this* place?'

6 Urban dreams: the birth of A Rocha UK

Anyone with any get-up-and-go has got up and gone from Southall.[1]
From *Bride and Prejudice*, written and directed by Gurinder Chadha, who grew up in Southall

I have it all planned out – plans to take care of you, not abandon you, plans to give you the future you hope for.[2]
God's promise to a people in exile in Babylon . . . and in Southall (Jeremiah 29:11).

For the first time, I began to wonder whether the twin passions Anne and I shared, for Southall and for A Rocha, could be combined. Was the urban wasteland I had been exploring a possible A Rocha site? It seemed such a crazy idea. Surely A Rocha was about beautiful, inspiring wild locations? Could it also be about the realities of urban living, of trying to balance the needs of people and wildlife in a place like London?

The more I thought about it, the more the idea of an urban A Rocha project grew on me. Living in Southall I'd become increasingly aware of the effect of an urban landscape upon local people. I came across a document produced by Southall Regeneration Partnership which said, 'There is a lack of greenery, open space, clean air and environmental awareness – all of which contribute to a lack of confidence and pride in the area.' I knew that Southall scored extremely highly in national statistics for mental illness, and that lack of access to green spaces was reckoned to be a contributing factor. And theologically this made sense to me. God made the first human beings to enjoy his company in a garden, amid the diversity and beauty of a creation that whispers God's name. The biblical story is certainly not against cities, for after all the final chapters of the Bible describe a heavenly city, but it is ultimately a garden city, a combination of God's creation and the best of human creativity. Our modern mega-cities often seem to be parasitic in the way they sustain their growth and greed by sucking resources and goodness out of the natural world, chewing them up and spitting them out in waste and pollution. Was a different vision possible, a sustainable city where nature was appreciated for its beauty and nurtured for its provision?

I was also acutely aware, as a local vicar, that the Christian churches in Southall were making little impact on the wider community. Here was a multi-faith town where Sikhs, Muslims and Hindus dominated, and the churches appeared to be an irrelevant relic of the past. This myth was destroyed once you met their vibrant multiracial congregations, but it remained the prevailing impression of Southall Christianity. However, what if Christians were at the heart of a project that benefited the whole community? What if the local environment was improved because of a vision of hope that came from the Christian faith? Could this help dissolve the myth that this was an irrelevant religion with nothing to say to twenty-first-century Londoners?

I began to visit the piece of land more regularly, walking and praying around it, and recording its wildlife through the year. I also started to research the site itself. The area, located between Southall and Hayes, turned out to be known as the

Minet site (more popularly the 'Minet Tip'), named after the family who'd originally owned the land. Long ago it would have been heath and farmland, lying between the hamlets of Southall and Hayes. Some of it was once water meadows grazed by cattle, and the lines of mature trees followed old field boundaries dating back several hundred years. When London grew, part of Minet was used for allotments; the northern end became a Victorian rubbish tip before being landscaped, and the strip between canal and river was used for decades to dump canal dredgings. After the Greater London Council was abolished, the main site's ownership transferred to the London Borough of Hillingdon, and since then it had been largely neglected, apart from a cycle circuit created at one end in the 1990s.

With growing interest, I made more enquiries, both locally and within the A Rocha family. At an A Rocha sup porters' day at Kew Gardens early in 1998 I gave a short presentation on possibilities in the UK, slipping in the idea of an urban project in Southall. I expected a negative reaction, knowing how many had visited Portugal and dreamed of a coastal paradise for A Rocha UK. But instead the supporters encouraged me to explore the idea further, saying this could be an important complement to A Rocha's work in Portugal. I met David Chandler, who worked for the RSPB and had written books on bird watching, and discovered that he had grown up in Hayes and learned his hobby on the Minet site! He even had lists of birds seen there in the 1970s – some like grey partridge and tree sparrow no longer present – and letters to the Greater London Council protesting at plans for a bypass destroying one edge of the site.

Speaking to local people, it became clear that there was a history around Minet of pressure to develop and build, prevented only by its greenbelt classification. And this isn't too surprising, for Minet is only fifteen minutes by car from Heathrow Airport, so the potential commercial value of a ninety-acre site like this was immense. Over the years it had gradually become degraded, not just from car boot sales, motorbike scrambling and burned-out cars, but by poor fencing which allowed illegal fly-tipping. One whole field was waist-deep in rubble, lorry tyres, asbestos roof tiles, old refrigerators and much more. Any project to clean this place up would be very costly, and would require a huge amount of co-ordination.

When I talked to British Waterways about the strip of land next to the canal, they pointed out that there was severe soil contamination: heavy metals and cyanides allegedly dumped decades previously from an adjacent gasworks. The millions it would cost to clean this up could be recovered only by a major development on the site. Removing the contamination would also destroy most of the wildlife habitats, at least temporarily. Perhaps this strip of land, sandwiched between the canal and the river, was best left as it was for now, protected by water, largely undisturbed by people, and already a wildlife haven?

Several people encouraged me to talk to the Member of Parliament for Hayes and Harlington, John McDonnell. When we met, I discovered that here was a real ally, somebody with the political knowledge, local connections, and above all the commitment to bring people together and achieve things. He proposed an informal forum of those with an interest in the site – councillors and officers from the London Borough of Hillingdon, local residents, groups using Hillingdon cycle circuit, the neighbouring Guru Nanak Sikh school, Yeading Football Club who leased a corner of the site for their ground, and Hayes Town Football Club, which, somewhat ominously, had proposals to build a large stadium on the Minet site. A Rocha were invited to be part of the discussions, representing the needs of nature conservation.

The first few meetings were pretty tense, with a lot of verbal shadow-boxing, testing out everyone's strength of feeling and support. Against my natural inclinations, I tried to keep quiet and listen, chipping in only to give evidence on the importance of keeping the site green for wildlife and local people. By now we'd talked to other conservation groups, such as London Wildlife Trust and Hillingdon Natural History Society. Both gave helpful information and encouraged A Rocha to speak for them in support of protecting Minet.

Suddenly things began moving quickly. I was still full-time vicar at St George's Southall, and A Rocha UK did not even exist legally – there was just an informal network of those supporting the work in Portugal. I talked things through with Peter Harris, who by now was International Director, and had moved from Portugal to France. A Rocha was becoming a truly international organization, with emerging projects in Lebanon, Kenya and France. Peter suggested we form a board of trustees and register A Rocha UK as a charity as soon as possible, and he encouraged me to think about moving on from my parish job to become founding Director of A Rocha UK.

Peter also put me in touch with John Smiley, who had just taken early retirement after a successful career in the business world. John lived in a prosperous area outside London, had never been to Southall in his life, and hated spicy food. Yet we were both Christians, enjoyed wildlife, and quickly felt that God had brought us together for this project. John became Chairman of A Rocha UK, and gradually other key people fell into place too, with skills in areas as diverse as conservation science, finance, charity governance, law and publicity. Crucially, these people were also all wise and prayerful. I then took the plunge and went to speak to Bishop Graham Dow, Bishop of Willesden, my 'boss' as a vicar. He was really helpful, initially urging me to see if I could combine A Rocha with parish work, but when I explained that I would need to preach for A Rocha around the UK, he agreed that I needed to be full-time.

It was only just beginning to sink in that, with three small children by now, we would be leaving the relative security of a vicar's job, with free housing and a stable income, for complete uncertainty. Where would we live? Who would pay us? What if it all went wrong and a vast football stadium or shopping complex was eventually built on the Minet site? I remember many sleepless nights, wondering if this wasn't just the most stupid thing I had ever embarked on.

If we were going to step into the unknown, then we needed some clear signs from God that it was right to go ahead. We had already received positive signals: the provision of John Smiley and the trustees, the 'co-incidence' of David Chandler's personal connection with the site, the role of John McDonnell in gathering people to discuss Minet's future. But we needed some more tangible signs – not anything dramatic like a big finger coming out of the sky saying, 'It's you – Go for it!', but basic things like practical voluntary help with the work, housing for when we moved out of the vicarage, and money to pay a salary. A small group of people from local churches had by now started meeting to pray about the emerging project, and we shared our needs with them. We also wrote to A Rocha's supporters around the UK.

Our first need was for somebody to do a thorough eco-logical survey of Minet, as my own expertise didn't go much beyond birds and butterflies. In response to our note to A Rocha's supporters, along came Colin Conroy, a somewhat unlikely angel with his corny jokes and his enormous appetite, but an angel nonetheless. Colin came to live with us for ten months, and he undertook a thorough survey of the Minet site. He paid his way by working nights, driving cars for a Heathrow parking company. When he eventually left us, it was to study for a master's degree in restoration ecology, how to repair damaged areas of land, a wonderfully relevant qualification.

As seems the case with many people who get involved, Colin has never quite managed to leave A Rocha. Over the following years he volunteered with us again, and became Conservation Officer for A Rocha UK once we could pay him. Later he felt God calling him to work for three years with A Rocha in Lebanon, and now, at the time of writing, has moved on to spend a year with A Rocha Canada. Caroline Park, an environmental attorney from Washington DC, took a sabbatical from her job and joined our emerging team. This was no holiday as she slogged away building up a database of local contacts for us and organizing much of the official launch. In time, Colin and Caroline would become close friends of ours, and godparents to our youngest daughter.

The second big sign we needed from God was an answer to our questions on accommodation. Vicarages come with the job, so we would need to move out and find a house locally – ideally somewhere big enough for a growing family, volunteers and an office – a big ask! We placed a cheeky notice in the A Rocha newsletter, asking if anybody fancied buying a property in Southall for us to live in. Amazingly, a supporter contacted us, offering to buy a house and rent it to A Rocha below the market rate, and even letting us choose the actual property. I was abroad when this happened, so Anne had the task of house hunting. Astonishingly, she found a five-bedroomed house near the station, with a long garden where an office could be built. Even more surprising was the discovery that the house was the former manse of a United Reformed church which had subsequently been rented by Southall Baptist Church. We sensed that this was far more than coincidence, but rather yet another sign of God at work, weaving his purposes through our often confused and clumsy decisions.

The final sign we needed was financial provision towards a salary, another big ask. The Bishop of London, Richard Chartres, already known for his positive environmental views, was very supportive, finding us significant grants for the first few years. I then went to see a friend who worked for the Church Mission Society, the mission my parents had worked with in India. Founded in 1799, CMS historically worked mainly in Asia and Africa. However, I knew that CMS was now also working in multiracial urban parts of the UK. After several interviews, endless forms and references, and assessments of our physical and mental health (surely we were certifiable for even thinking of a project like this?), CMS took Anne and me on as mission partners. This meant they would give a grant each year towards our costs. While we were still short of funding for the first year, let alone beyond, we felt that this was the final piece of the jigsaw, confirming God's leading to launch out full-time with A Rocha at the start of 2001.

* * *

If we were going to have an A Rocha project in Southall and Hayes, then we had to have a name for it. We wanted a name that conveyed something about transforming the environment while subtly implying our Christian basis. As we tried out all sorts of imaginative and a few unrepeatable ideas, it was a map of the Minet site that eventually triggered inspiration. The site itself was surrounded on three sides by water: Yeading Brook, the Grand Union Canal, and a man-made flood relief channel flowing into the brook. Anne asked, 'How about A Rocha Living Waterways?' It was a name that spoke about the site, implied abundant natural life, and had strong biblical links. I was reminded of Ezekiel 47, where the prophet sees a new river of life flowing out from God's temple, a river that cleanses barren, dried-out places and brings fresh life wherever it goes. It's a passage that Jesus probably had in mind when he said, 'Let anyone who is thirsty come to me and drink' (John 7:37). So we agreed: 'A Rocha Living Waterways', seeking 'a greener, cleaner Southall and Hayes'.

We decided to launch the project officially in February 2001. Meanwhile we discovered that Anne was pregnant again. One Sunday morning, early in the pregnancy, I was at home preparing for the service at St George's when I heard a terrifying scream. Anne was losing blood rapidly and had clearly suffered a huge internal haemorrhage. Leaving my colleague Sue Jelfs to start the service, I rushed Anne to the hospital. We were whisked through Accident and Emergency, and the doctors did their best to stem the bleeding and stop Anne from falling unconscious. From worried faces and whispered words, I gathered that not only the baby but also Anne herself was at risk due to losing so much blood. Eventually, after what seemed forever but was actually less than an hour, Anne was relatively stable, so I raced back to St George's, swapping places with Sue, who, as a trained midwife, was the perfect person to be with Anne. I don't know how I got through the rest of the service. It was a baptism with communion, and praying God's blessing on somebody else's new baby when I thought we had just lost our own child was heartbreaking, but somehow I was given the strength to carry on.

A few days after Anne was stabilized and back at home, the hospital called her in for a scan. While they were sure that the baby had been lost during the haemorrhage, they wanted to check whether Anne needed any further internal procedures. We went together, both still traumatized by the whole experience, and hoping Anne would not need surgery. When the scan began, there was a pause, and then the nurse turned to us: 'You do know that you are pregnant, don't you?' There, on the small screen, was a tiny but clear heartbeat. What a mix of feelings: disbelief, joy, nervous concern. This baby was clearly a fighter, and to us yet another reminder that God can bring hope out of apparently hopeless situations. When she was eventually born, we called her Naomi-Ruth, partly as a reminder of the biblical story of two women to whom God remained faithful throughout very tough times.

A close examination of the pregnancy showed that the placenta was partially detached, so Anne was put on strict bedrest for the next six months. I now had a bed-ridden wife, three children aged five and under, a parish to run, a project launch to oversee, and the small matter of moving house. It was certainly a test of our resolve. Friends and family rallied around, cooking meals, decorating the new house, looking after the children. Generous friends paid for Rosie, just eighteen months old, to go to a private day nursery, and later for a wonderful German au pair, Gabriela, to help us out. Nevertheless, our lives felt like the new house – a chaotic, confused jumble. Not surprisingly, we were both very low: totally unsure that setting up A Rocha UK was the right thing to do. It wasn't exactly a promising beginning.

Then, at long last, 1 February 2001 arrived, the day of A Rocha UK's launch celebration. We held it at Blair Peach Primary School, just across the canal from the Minet site, and also the school which our older daughters attended. One of our new trustees, Debbie Wright, who had worked for the BBC, insisted that we have a high-profile launch. I didn't sleep at all the previous night – there was so much that could go wrong, and I had no sense of peace.

But in the end, the day went like a dream. More than three hundred people turned up: A Rocha supporters from around the country joining parents from the school, leaders from local faith groups, family and friends. Among the supporters I was amazed to see people who had taught me at Monkton Combe, and nurtured both my Christian faith and my love for nature. The launch made the front page of the local paper, and even BBC London turned up to film it.

The programme included Indian dancing and singing by the children. There was amazing food, cooked and served by a friend, Jamian, aided by his sister and friends. We heard powerful speeches from John McDonnell MP, who spoke warmly of A Rocha's work, and from Sir Ghillean Prance (former Director of Kew Gardens), who spoke about his passion for plants and for Jesus. There was a short walk around the Minet site, and one elderly lady spoke of how this project gave her, after fifty years of Christian faith, a new insight into the meaning of redemption.

Finally we held a service of worship and commissioning back at the school. The musicians had not met until that morning, yet the music came together, and there was a sense of heaven touching earth as we were lifted into God's presence in worship. Anne had rested all week so she could be there, and we stood together as people gathered around, placed their hands on us and commissioned us for this new project. We felt weak, unconfident and ill-equipped, yet also completely surrounded by the love and prayers of many people, resting on a God who specializes in bringing order out of chaos.

7 The vision unfolds

I used to assume that the direction of 'progress' was somehow inevitable, not to be questioned. I passively accepted a new road through the middle of the park, a steel and glass bank where a two-hundred-year-old church had stood, and the fact that life seemed to get harder and faster each day. I do not any more . . . I have seen that community and a close relationship with the land can enrich human life beyond all comparison with material wealth or technological sophistication. I have learned that another way is possible.[1]

Greg Mortenson, former mountain climber who now builds schools in rural northern Pakistan and Afghanistan

The problem with mountain tops is that there's nowhere to go but down. After the wonderful launch of A Rocha Living Waterways, suddenly it was all official. People had expectations of us and the pressure was on. I would be stopped in the street by people asking how it was going. I was tempted to reply 'How's *what* going?', because there wasn't much to report. The Minet site was still a mess, the council was not yet committed to our vision for the site, and the dream of a wonderful new park still seemed a fantasy. I wasn't a vicar any more, I was 'Director of A Rocha UK', but in practice all it meant was that instead of working from a nice warm study in a large vicarage, I was working from a small, cold, wooden shed-office at the bottom of the garden. I had no team, for our key volunteers, Colin and Caroline, had both had to move on. Anne was still on complete bedrest with a fragile pregnancy. As 2001 progressed, the project's finances ran lower and lower until at one point we had only just over one month's salary in the bank. On many occasions I wondered whether it was all a big mistake.

It was not the first or the last time that I've found uncertainty and potential failure to be part of the normal Christian life. As we step out on a limb with God, there are no guarantees that we won't fall off. I'm taken back to the story of Jesus inviting Peter to get out of the boat and walk on water. It's a scary business, especially if you're a practical fisherman with a healthy respect for the sea. We can easily visualize everything that might go wrong and start to sink below the waves. But Jesus is there and he uses hard experiences to stretch our faith and increase our dependence on him. We may take our eyes off Jesus, but he never takes his eyes off us. He lets us flail around looking stupid, but he never lets us drown.

By nature I am an activist, and if nothing was happening I would try to make it happen. I rushed around filling my diary with meetings, whipping up support by speaking to local schools and churches, lobbying politicians, writing letters and emails, or looking for rare wildlife that might guarantee the Minet site's protection. It took me a very long time to realize deep down that this was God's project, not mine, and that however hard I worked I couldn't make it happen by myself. There was just no way that a former vicar with no environmental qualifications could overturn thirty years of neglect on Minet or raise the millions of pounds needed to transform it.

Every now and then something would happen that forcibly reminded me that this was in fact God's project.

While I believe in miracles (after Anne's healing I didn't have much choice!), I have to admit that they always take me by surprise. Sometimes they can be very small things. On one occasion, towards the end of 2001, I was rushing around, late and disorganized, getting materials together for an after-school environment club we'd started in a local primary school. The children were all typical, urban, Southall kids – mainly Sikh, Hindu and Muslim. When we began the club, they were terrified of touching the soil – 'Ugh, it's dirty!' – and when we found a worm, they would run away screaming, thinking it was a snake. Now, after three months, they'd moved from fear of nature to curiosity and wonder. They were a great group, and this was the last club before the Christmas holidays. I wanted to give them a treat – an impromptu Christmas party. The only problem was that I hadn't planned ahead: we only had a couple of packets of crisps in the house and it was too late to go to the shops. Rushing out of the front door, I prayed, 'Please help this not to be a total disaster – I really want the kids to have a good time and to know how special Christmas is.' I slammed the door, and as I did so saw a plastic box on the doorstep, nearly missing it in my hurry. Inside was a chocolate cake, an unexpected gift from Kay, a member of our church. That cake made it a very special Christmas party for the kids at the after-school club that year. To me it was also a special, gentle reminder from God that this was his project, not mine, and that he was in charge. God can and does speak today through chocolate cakes.

During the early years we had a couple of other remarkable 'coincidences', which served to remind us, during the difficult times, of God's oversight. A few months into 2001, we advertised for an administrator, as the work was rapidly becoming more than I could handle alone, and Deborah, our temporary part-time help, had had to move on. When we interviewed, the obvious candidate was Sarah Leedham who had wide and varied experience of environmental work, had grown up locally, and shared our Christian vision. However she would need accommodation, and there was no way she could rent a flat in Southall on what we could afford to pay her. Nevertheless we offered her the job and promised to help her find somewhere local to live. Within five minutes of offering her the job, I went down to the garden shed-office and discovered an answerphone message. To my astonishment, it was from a member of our local church asking if we needed a small house in Southall. Somebody she knew in New Zealand had inherited it from a relative, didn't want to sell for a while, and was happy to have it lived in at a nominal rent. Of course this could have been coincidental: 'just one of those things', but the timing and our need for God's reassurance in those fragile early days of the work made me think otherwise.

Even more extraordinary is the story of the bread-maker. Anne wanted a bread-maker, not only for our family, but because our house was the centre of the project, and there's nothing like warm, home-baked bread to create a community atmosphere. Sharing food is a core value in A Rocha, and at lunchtimes our growing team would be joined by volunteers, visitors and anybody else who was around. We decided that we couldn't buy just a small family-sized bread-maker – we had to go for a much larger one so that everybody could enjoy fresh bread at lunch. The only problem was that it would cost a princely sum – £100 more than the smaller one. We swallowed hard and bought it, feeling this was part of our commitment to community living. A week later we hosted an A Rocha prayer meeting, attended by several people from local churches. Nothing was said about the bread-maker, but afterwards we had a letter from Margaret Barlow, who'd attended. Margaret wrote hesitantly, saying she wasn't used to God speaking to her but had sensed in the meeting that God wanted her to give us some money 'for a bread-maker'. Her cheque was for £100. Anne and I stood in our kitchen choking back tears, as we marvelled at a God who was not only big enough to hold the whole universe together, but personal enough to assure us that he was with us even in the smallest things.

As I've reflected on these early encouragements, I have come to see that God gave us these small, yet to us very significant, miracles in order to prepare us for the bigger battles to come. For the more we learned about the story of the Minet site, the crazier our vision seemed to become. We found that there had been various plans to develop the site over the years, and ninety acres of prime real estate situated near the M4 motorway and Heathrow Airport were not going to be saved without a fight. While greenbelt classification meant that Minet was theoretically protected from development for housing or business, there were various groups with their eyes on the land, as mentioned earlier, for a football or athletics stadium. Often local people who'd known the area for years would smile knowingly when I shared our vision. 'Best of luck!' they'd say, but I could see what they were thinking: 'Nothing ever changes around here – there are just too many vested interests.' From the meetings with the local MP, the council and other interested parties, I knew that reaching an agreement wouldn't be easy. Some of the council officers had begun to draw up plans showing what a country park could look like, and it made me realize what a huge project this was. Even if we got approval, it was going to cost well over a million pounds to clean up the site, put in some landscaping and fencing, and plant it with trees. Where was all that going to come from?

Every time I went to a meeting, I knew it could be the final one. The council might suddenly decide to stop talking to us, either because they had other plans, or because they didn't want to be associated with a Christian group, or because they simply couldn't see how we could fund it. We knew of one significant source of available money: a government 'Single Regeneration Budget' fund already allocated to the area. More funding was needed, though. Then came a break-through, and again I can only put this down to God's working.

Some years previously, a Sainsbury's supermarket had been built on the original Minet estate. As part of the planning agreement, the council had been paid a huge sum in compensation to be spent on local environmental improvements. As I read about this, I was confused as to where most of the money had gone. Some had helped build the excellent cycle circuit on part of Minet, but I could find nothing about where the rest of it had been spent. Although I was puzzled, I didn't see what I could do about it. However, I wasn't the only one asking questions. John McDonnell MP persisted until the council were forced to undergo a district auditor's enquiry. To everybody's aston-ishment, hundreds of thousands of pounds were found in a 'forgotten account'. When I heard this, I remember a tingle going down my spine. To me it was just another piece in the jigsaw, showing us this was God's project.

The final chunk of major funding came as an inspired sug-gestion from one of Hillingdon Council's planning officers. Under UK law all waste must be disposed of through a licensed landfill site – and businesses pay heavily to get rid of it. However, if the soil or rubble from a building site is certified as 'clean' – free of any pollutants – then, instead of going to landfill, another landowner can be paid to take it at a lower cost. All of us were in agreement that some areas of the Minet site had been so badly damaged by misuse that they were of no real ecological value, and would have to be completely re-landscaped and re-planted. So why not agree to accept, and be paid for, tens of thousands of tons of clean soil and rubble from local building sites, and landscape it into some new 'hills'? As a result, if you visit the Minet site today you will find several small rounded hills covered in grass and trees. In fact, if you scrape away the topsoil, you'll find the remains of much of the old Wembley Stadium, which was being redeveloped just as we started. So, from the hallowed turf of Wembley to the hallowed hills of Minet!

But we're getting ahead of ourselves. Discussions about a proposed country park on Minet continued throughout 2001, and A Rocha worked with Groundwork Thames Valley on a major community consultation which showed over-whelming support for the site to be cleaned up, made safe, and kept as open space for local people.

The weekly wildlife walks continued, and more and more species of bird, butterfly and dragonfly were being recorded on the site. By 2001 over ninety species of bird had been recorded, mainly by Colin Conroy and me, and we'd even discovered breeding kingfishers. In the summer of 2001, while much of England was out of bounds due to foot and mouth disease, Minet was clear because we had no livestock, and a research student from Oxford came to look at some temporary ponds. To our surprise, she found several nation-ally rare species of water beetle! All in all, things were looking good, and every time I walked around the site I had a real sense of excitement.

Then came disaster. In December 2001 the London Borough of Hillingdon finally submitted its own planning application to turn Minet into a country park. It was a document we'd worked on together for many months; we were pleased with it, and everyone turned out to the council meeting at which it was to be approved. But at the crucial meeting on 18 April 2002 it became clear that not everybody shared the same vision. Despite all the work, the planning decision was postponed on a technicality. Rumours were flying around about links with a football club and secret plans to build a huge stadium. The atmosphere was one of confrontation, hidden agendas and, in several people's opinion, spiritual warfare.

Confused and worried, I drove home and went to bed. During the night, I had a strong sense that this was indeed a spiritual battle. If it was God's plan for the Minet site to be rescued and restored, then there were also forces at work trying to prevent this. I am not prone to finding demons in every corner, but as a minister I've seen enough of the effects of evil to take it very seriously when I do encounter it.

Much of the greatest evil in today's world is institutional – tied up in worshipping the false gods of money and power – and it was the smell of such attitudes that I sensed that evening.

The most effective weapons in a spiritual battle are spiritual ones, and prayer is the most powerful. So, with six weeks until the council reconsidered the planning application for Minet Country Park, we needed to marshal as much prayer as possible. As an A Rocha team we walked around Minet, praying for God's protection and healing on the land. We emailed A Rocha supporters near and far, and I also wrote to the Bishop of Willesden, by that time Pete Broadbent, asking if he would forward a request to local churches to pray about the planning decision. I suggested church members might like to write to their local councillors giving their views on the value of protecting Minet.

Those six weeks felt like an eternity, and they were full of uncertainty. Once again deep-rooted fears surfaced: what if it all went wrong? What if I'd only been imagining that God was with us? I had to hang on tightly to the clear evidence of God's leading and the answers to prayer we'd already had. Eventually the next planning meeting came along. My diary records:

> On 30th May the planning committee met again in a totally different atmosphere. Councillors from all parties spoke strongly in favour of the country park and we were granted permission for work to begin. Amid the celebrations and

relief, we reflected on what had happened during the roller-coaster six weeks of uncertainty. At one level we had acted in lobbying and writing letters. At another level politicians had reconsidered the wisdom of refusing a project with extensive public support and public funding, and the football club had not submitted an application, for their own reasons, which we may never know. At yet another level, many people had prayed, with unseen but tangible effect. Now the Minet Country Park project is moving ahead, with A Rocha UK providing ecological advice and monitoring, and we hope to report on the new park being opened in mid-2003 . . . hopefully without any more giant roller coasters!

Once again, just as we felt we were about to sink beneath the waves, God had come to our rescue. In mid-2002, as I looked back on eighteen months of A Rocha Living Waterways, I could only marvel. A dream had now become a real project. I thought back to late 1997, when I'd first sensed God asking: 'How do you think I feel about this place?' Now I was beginning to sense how God felt. God cares for his earth with the passion of a parent. He notices when even a single sparrow falls to the ground. His heart breaks when we pollute and destroy with our carelessness. And he rejoices when we catch his vision, and work with him to restore and renew his creation.

8 The miracle of Minet

The desolate land will be cultivated instead of lying desolate in the sight of all who pass through it. They will say, 'This land that was laid waste has become like the garden of Eden; the cities that were lying in ruins, desolate and destroyed, are now fortified and inhabited.' Then the nations around you that remain will know that I the LORD have rebuilt what was destroyed and have replanted what was desolate. I the LORD have spoken, and I will do it.
Ezekiel 36:34–36

Once planning permission had been granted, it was full steam ahead. A tight timetable was agreed by the council, contractors were appointed, and the diggers rolled in. Colin Conroy became Project Ecologist, ensuring that the ecologically sensitive areas were not disturbed, and that landscaping and replanting were done to create the best possible mosaic of wildlife habitats.

Some of the rubbish was large and had to be dealt with by specialists – tons of hardcore that had surfaced the car boot sale area, and perhaps fifteen burned-out cars scattered across the site. However, much of it was smaller and spread amongst fields full of wildlife. Ancient hedgerows concealed piles of car tyres, and one particular field, classified as 'Ancient Middlesex Meadowland', was waist-deep in fly-tipping: an ugly mixture of rubble, roofing tiles, old refrigerators, and bits of metal and glass. But we didn't want heavy earth-moving machinery in here, for it would have damaged and destroyed important, fragile wildlife habitats.

We spoke to the council and, with their agreement, organized working parties to clear whatever we could into massive piles on the edge of the field. Looking back, it was one of the best things we did, because it involved so many different local people, all of whom got to know and appreciate Minet. On various occasions we had Christians, Muslims, conservation volunteers, young offenders – people of various ages, abilities and ethnic backgrounds. There is nothing better than working together on a physical project to build community, and that was certainly how it felt. On some days we would hear woodpeckers drumming in the trees and skylarks singing above, see butterflies resting in sunny corners, and perhaps a vole or shrew scurrying away from a pile we were clearing. There was a sense of putting right an ancient wrong, of helping create the conditions for life to be fruitful, even of God saying as he did at the beginning, 'And it is very good.'

On one occasion, a businessman offered to send a mechanical digger to clear the piles of rubbish. We got chatting to the driver and he asked what we were doing. We told him the story and he gave a wry smile. Some years before he'd worked as a driver for a different employer who'd told him to save money by dumping truckloads of waste on the site. Now here he was helping to clear it up!

Gradually the site was cleared. Colin advised us to leave some piles of wood and rubble in out-of-the-way places to create habitats for reptiles and small mammals. We even disturbed a grass snake on a couple of occasions, slithering away from the warmth of its hiding place. Our wildlife list continued to grow as the site gradually improved: the old oaks in the hedgerows harboured small numbers of the elusive purple hairstreak butterfly, the channels and ponds housed frogs and newts, and several species of bat flew around at night. We realized that Minet was something of an oasis in the urban desert, for migrating birds often follow watercourses and, with Yeading Brook, the Grand Union Canal and the flood-relief channel, the area was sometimes like a busy motorway intersection. As time went on, we recorded different warblers in the spring and summer: some years grasshopper warblers hid in damp grassland, their monotonous 'fishing reel' song the only clue to their whereabouts. In autumn and spring many birds passed through on their way to and from their breeding sites. One spring a nightingale sang for two nights before moving on, and on other occasions someone spotted a cuckoo. Wheatears, whinchats, redstarts, pied and spotted fly-catchers all came and went in spring or autumn, and – most unexpectedly of all – one September a wryneck appeared for four days, a bizarre-looking member of the woodpecker family, with a beautiful grey, brown and buff plumage and a habit of turning its head in an almost-full circle. Our wryneck stayed for four days and produced Minet's first 'twitch', as birdwatchers from across London and beyond came to see it. As I write this, improved management and recording have led the total of bird species on Minet to climb to over 120, not bad for an inland urban site with no major lakes or marshes.

But I'm getting ahead of myself. During 2002–2003 we saw more big yellow trucks than rare birds, as thousands of cubic metres of rubble and soil were brought on to the site. Things looked far worse before they started to improve, as most of Minet became a sea of mud. But eventually, order emerged from the chaos, and new hills or 'bunds' began to take shape. Some were covered in topsoil and left unseeded so that native plants could re-establish themselves. One was left completely bare of topsoil, to discourage the weedy plants that like fertile soil and encourage other less dominant species. Others were planted with a mix of grass and wild-flower seed. When spring arrived, Minet was suddenly a blaze of scarlet poppies and blue cornflowers.

Strong gates and wooden fencing were erected to prevent further dumping or motorcycle scrambling and to give a parkland feel. The rubbish-filled pond was cleared, greatly enlarged and, after a wet winter, was soon full again. Further down the channel that led from the pond to Yeading Brook, two small weirs were put in place. These would hold water in the channel through the dryness of summer, and they also create new ponds – and they've become very popular with school groups!

Our plans to host visiting groups from schools and else-where would need a building as a base: somewhere with toilets, a small kitchen and office, and an indoor classroom to retreat to if it got wet. The council's solution was what looked like a rustic wooden cabin, but was actually a solid steel, vandal-proof box, covered with wood. It was named 'Minet Lodge', and has since become the base for our Community Liaison Officer, as well as for all sorts of local events that A Rocha organizes. Next to it, as the lorries retreated, a car park and an adventure playground were created on the former car-boot sale area.

Throughout, we tried to ensure that the local community felt they 'owned' the new park – that they had a say in and helped to create it. For decades Minet had been largely a no-go area except for vandals and bikers. If local people were to start using it again, they needed to feel it was not just the council's project, but their own local park. We especially wanted young people to be involved. Not only was it a great place to discover, but if they'd helped to create it, they were less likely to destroy it!

Once the landscaping was complete, we organized a massive community tree-planting exercise. It would have been simpler and possibly cheaper to appoint a contractor, but Hillingdon Council saw the long-term sense of involving local young people. Large numbers of children from schools and Scout groups came and planted thousands of new trees and shrubs, all from native stock, following a plan that A Rocha helped to design. Inevitably not all the trees have survived, but the majority are growing strongly and already providing good habitats for wildlife. When local children come down to the park, they can see how these trees and shrubs are doing, and feel a sense of connection with all that is happening.

At last, as summer 2003 approached, we began to plan a grand opening celebration for Minet Country Park. We sent out invitations to local faith leaders, the Mayor of Ealing, and John McDonnell MP, as well as to all those who had worked and prayed for the site. We were delighted that some patient detective work uncovered a certain Mr Paul Minet and his wife, descendants of the family who had owned the site many years before, and after whom it was named. We wanted a guest speaker who shared our Christian and environmental commitment, and would go down well with our multiracial London audience. We found the perfect person in Ram Gidoomal, a successful businessman and entrepreneur within the Asian community, who had become a Christian after arriving in Britain, and who chaired the London Sustainability Commission.

Two days before the big celebration, Colin Conroy was walking around Minet when something colourful caught his eye on the bare soil next to the pond. A discarded crisp packet perhaps? No! It was a bee orchid, a member of the most unusual and beautiful family of flowers. Nobody we talked to had any previous records of orchids on Minet. Perhaps its spores had lain in the soil for years, unable to develop and flower because of all the undergrowth and rubbish. However, the freshly disturbed soil was perfect for bee orchids. That's the biological explanation, but for those of us who'd been involved in the project, this was more than just a flower: it was a symbol of new life and new hope. After many years of being choked by rubbish and neglect, the Minet site was beginning to thrive again. The God who created everything from nothing was giving us one more sign of his commitment to restoring this good place.

With such an unexpected and wonderful symbolic centre-piece, the opening celebrations were a day to remember. On 14 June 2003 the sun shone warmly, hundreds of people from near and far turned out, and local children performed a specially produced play. Jamian, who'd catered for our launch two and a half years earlier, prepared an amazing buffet, and everybody poured out of the hall in groups to walk around the new country park, and of course to see the bee orchid. Finally there was a service of thanksgiving and celebration. Ram Gidoomal spoke about how God rebuilds what we have destroyed: lives, communities and creation. I was struck by the words Ram read from Ezekiel 36:34–36, God's words of restoration and blessing to Israel in exile. Yet they are also words linked to God's new covenant which Christians see as fulfilled in Jesus, and thus their promise is universal:

> The desolate land will be cultivated instead of lying desolate in the sight of all who pass through it. They will say, 'This land that was laid waste has become like the garden of Eden; the cities that were lying in ruins, desolate and destroyed, are now fortified and inhabited.' Then the nations around you that remain will know that I the LORD have rebuilt what was destroyed and have replanted what was desolate. I the LORD have spoken, and I will do it.

Against the odds, Minet had become a wonderful visual reminder that nothing is beyond God's power to transform. Jesus talked about signs, foretastes, of God's future kingdom amongst us in the here and now. To us Minet had become a sign of the kingdom, of the healing of the land (2 Chronicles 7:14). That does not mean that Minet will be as it is now for eternity. Signs are pointers to something that is still to come. They lift your eyes and give you hope that you are en route to your destination. Just as God healing somebody physically is a 'sign of the kingdom', even though that person may die later, so the healing of Minet had become a signpost to the coming kingdom of God.

Once this was a barren wasteland, a place people avoided, a symbol of humanity's greed and wastefulness. But with God, nothing is wasted. Now it was restored, renewed, and in a real sense it had begun to be redeemed. My prayer was that this wouldn't just be an end in itself, but would inspire others to look again at places where they lived. If God could transform the wasteland of Minet, then surely nowhere – and nobody – is beyond his power to redeem or restore.

9 A team and a centre

*This is something God is doing and it is a sign of hope, and the
secular environmental people recognize this more than the
Christians! If God's people will live faithfully in response to Jesus
the Lord, there is hope for the planet, just as there is hope for
people's lives and hope for human societies.*[1]
Peter Harris, Founder and President of A Rocha
International

In order to give a personal perspective on the Minet story, I
have underplayed the most important element. The transformation of Minet was never about one individual or couple
and their ideas and work. It was always, and increasingly as
time went on, a team effort in every possible way. For A Rocha
was just one partner in redeveloping Minet, working with
the council, the MP, the cyclists, local schools, sports clubs
and neighbourhood groups. In addition, the A Rocha UK team
grew rapidly during 2001–2003, both in terms of staff and
volunteers.

When I stepped out of full-time church-based ministry,
I had little experience of managing projects or finances.
The small group of trustees were immensely helpful, and
John Smiley as Chairman particularly threw his energy
into making sure that A Rocha UK was financially and

organizationally sound. It was our plan gradually to build a project team, as we found the funding and the right people.

The very first member of the team was my wife, Anne. Once our youngest daughter Naomi-Ruth arrived safely in May 2001, Anne became part-time Team Leader, concentrating on welcoming visitors and volunteers, coordinating team meals, and exercising a pastoral role within and beyond the project. Her biggest contribution though was in the area of ideas and advice. Anne shares my passion for Southall, for God's creation, for the Minet site, and for A Rocha's ethos. Everything I've done has been done jointly with her. Her wisdom has prevented my sillier ideas from seeing the light of day, and has refined others until they make more sense! However, although immensely capable, Anne has always felt that her prime calling is to bring up our children, and so we needed to look to others to build our A Rocha team.

The first need in 2001 was for a full-time administrator, as I was away from the office so much. Sarah Leedham, whom we met earlier, would have much preferred hands-on practical conservation outdoors, but patiently sat in the office dealing with phone calls, emails and endless paperwork. When Minet was fully open as a country park, she would get her chance as a Community Liaison Officer, but there was no promise of that when she joined us in 2001.

Next came our education officers. We'd always planned that A Rocha Living Waterways would have three main areas of work: practical wildlife conservation at Minet, community projects creating a wider sustainability agenda among faith groups in Southall and Hayes, and environmental education through local schools. The last of these proved easiest to obtain grant funding for, and hard work in fund-raising was rewarded with two major three-year grants. This was enormously exciting for us: further evidence that, as a new, small Christian charity, people were prepared to back us. After advertising and interviewing, we appointed two Education

Officers: Rachel Woods, a talented artist with a teaching background, and Jonathan Nicholas, who had been working at an outdoor education centre delivering environmental education.

I had started one after-school environment club, and done assemblies in various schools, but with Rachel and Jonathan we were able to expand this work considerably. Primary schools welcomed A Rocha with open arms, seeing that we were providing something that was lacking locally. Gradually a schools package developed, and has since continued to evolve, initially with termly assemblies taking a different environmental theme and reaching thousands of children. After-school clubs were started in several local primary schools, as was a summer programme of field visits to Minet Country Park, where a variety of activities linked to the national curriculum were on offer.

Right from the start, the feedback from both pupils and staff has been enthusiastic. Many local children had never previously visited a park of any kind. We even had parents worried about whether their kids would be safe from 'wild animals' at Minet! It was rewarding simply to see the excitement of children running up and down Minet's new 'mountains', showing one another spiders and butterflies in the long grass, or dipping into a pond and finding water snails or dragonfly larvae. During summer holidays we were able to work with children and their families more informally. Each year we ran week-long playschemes, often one based at Minet and one on a local housing estate. In these we were freer to explore wider themes and, very gently and with parents' permission, to explore our understanding that this world is not just beautiful, but created by a loving, caring God who wants us to know him and to care for his world.

And for me this is core to what life is all about. We are created to relate to God's creation, placed within a garden to tend and care for it, and impoverished when we lose contact with nature. If you've never eaten food you've grown yourself, never seen the stars in the night sky owing to light pollution, never been alone in a wilderness area, then is it surprising that you don't appreciate nature? Today experts increasingly speak about the importance of linking urban and rural areas, and the growing gap between them. In a small way, our work with environmental education in Southall and Hayes has sought to bridge that gap.

As I've seen the positive impact of a deeper relationship with nature in children's lives, a personal dream has emerged: that every primary school should give children an opportunity to grow food, to experience the weeding, planting, nurturing, waiting and harvesting, and also that every secondary school child should have a 'wilderness experience' – a time away from reliance on gadgets, cars and noise, experiencing our total dependence on nature. These experiences could be profound times, individually and culturally transformative, in terms of restoring our broken relationship with God's world.

On a few occasions we've had trips beyond Southall, introducing urbanized groups of children to the countryside and wildlife. For our 'Amazing Creation' week in Cornwall in 2003, we camped in the garden of A Rocha supporters Anthony and Pauline Hereward. It was an action-packed, pond-dipping, badger-watching, rock-pooling, eclipse-gazing, woodland-walking, sea-swimming week. Some of the reactions were wonderful: 'Yuk it's salty!' on first tasting seawater! To learn about our dependence on God's creation, we spent a day on an organic farm, visited an alternative energy centre and the tropical biome at the Eden Project.

Sir Ghillean Prance, whom we met earlier, is both Chairman of A Rocha International and also Scientific Director at the Eden Project. He offered to show us around the 'tropical biome', explaining from his own experience of crash-landing in the jungle how we are completely dependent on plants and can find food, water, shelter, medicine and materials from them. At one point he stopped and pointed to an obscure South American plant. 'This is very important,' he said, 'we've discovered that it contains a chemical that we can use to treat childhood leukaemia.' What Sir Ghillean didn't know was that one of the boys in the group had a younger brother who was prevented from joining us because he was undergoing treatment for leukaemia. It was a vivid illustration of our total reliance on God's creation, and of the dangers posed by destroying it.

Each evening, after cooking, eating and washing-up, we would gather in the Herewards' lounge to reflect with the children on their day. The experiences were so intense that there was an atmosphere of wonder and thankfulness. Perhaps it's not surprising that, years later, we are still in touch with many of those children and their families.

* * *

Meanwhile, back in London, Andy McCullough, a local Christian with an environmental degree and a vision for community transformation, turned his hand to everything from clearing rubbish to improving our financial systems, to building relationships with faith leaders in Hayes and Southall. He became so indispensable that eventually we scraped together the resources to pay him, and so Andy became our first Community Projects Officer. An important part of this role was to build bridges between A Rocha and the hugely diverse, multi-faith community.

We set up Southall Sustainability Forum, to which leaders from across the community were invited. The meetings sought to highlight issues of local concern and look at them from the perspective of sustainability. We would discuss transport (Southall has terrible traffic jams), or rats and rubbish (another contentious local issue), seek to find common ground, and then go to the local council with an action plan. On one memorable occasion we brought a collection of faith leaders together on a boat on the Grand Union Canal between Southall and Hayes to hammer out an agreed statement on 'Creation Care'. The great advantage of the boat was that, once we set off, nobody could walk away! After much discussion we produced an agreed form of words in which we stated that, whatever our other differences, all our faiths taught that the earth is created by God and is to be looked after carefully and reverently.

Sometimes people have questioned why a Christian organization works so closely with other religions. Is there not a danger we might lose our focus, or water down our Christian commitment by doing so? Nothing could be further from the truth. If anything, the more time I spend working with those of other faiths, the more I have found my own faith strengthened. The Bible, and therefore Christian thinking, begins not with Jesus but with God's creation of the earth, its creatures, and humanity. The call to care for the earth is given not only to Christians or even just to people of faith – it is a universal calling on all human beings to work together as good stewards of creation. Furthermore, as we work together we discover that the things that unite us are often greater than those that divide us. We all have to share God's world. We are all guilty of polluting and over-consuming, and we need to find shared values in building a more sustainable future. This does not mean Christians compromising their faith in Christ. Rather, it has been our experience that environmental work provides foundations of friendship between faiths, on which understanding can be built, and genuine sharing of what we believe and why can take place.

Within eighteen months of launching A Rocha UK, our team had grown to six, and then seven when Colin Conroy rejoined us. Our 'garden shed' headquarters was overflowing and, although we rented an extra office in a local church, we were often too numerous to fit around our table at lunchtimes. It was obvious that, sooner or later, we were going to need larger premises.

* * *

When Anne and I dreamed about A Rocha UK, we always imagined a purpose-built centre. We'd been inspired by community life at Cruzinha, A Rocha Portugal's centre, where we'd seen team members, volunteers and visitors living under one roof, sharing their lives in and out of working hours. We knew from our own experiences at St George's vicarage that living in community is no easy dream, but believed that it was an important statement both of our ecological values (sharing resources) and of our Christian witness (the transforming welcome we find in God). Our dream was to have a state-of-the-art, eco-friendly building, using the best in sustainable building materials, energy-saving technology, and low-carbon energy production. We would grow our own food, recycle our waste water and try to set an example by our lifestyles. The building would house offices, classrooms, a large community space, and flexible accommodation upstairs. We even sat down with the team and a retired architect to put the vision on paper. As we looked at maps of Southall and Hayes, we also formed ideas of exactly where the centre should go. Just across the canal from Minet, in the heart of Southall, is a huge redundant gasworks. Our vision was of a centre on a corner of this brownfield site, right next to existing housing and a primary school, and just across the canal from Minet, to which it would be linked by a new footbridge.

Sometimes visions come to fruition, and sometimes they have to be reshaped. As we discussed our ideas on community with the rest of the team, it was clear that not everybody fully shared them, for the team included introverts who needed plenty of space as well as noisy extroverts. Some felt called to community living, but others didn't. For Anne and me, the A Rocha vision was all-encompassing, bringing together everything that our lives and our faith were about. I found it very hard to understand that not everybody saw it the same way. For me this was not a job – it was a calling, and I happily worked extra hours in the evenings and at weekends. Others however supported A Rocha's vision, but their passion might be for their local church and their involvement in music or youth work there. Initially I expected that everybody would want to eat together not only at lunchtimes mid-week, but also one or two evenings a week, and to meet for prayer and Bible study together as well. Slowly I realized that I was trying to impose an unrealistic model, without letting others help shape the vision. I became confused, hurt, and sometimes angry with other team members, feeling they weren't pulling their weight. Very gradually I saw that, however clear my vision was, if it wasn't a vision others shared, then who was I to claim it was God's?

Much the same painful process happened with finding an A Rocha centre. I was holding out for the impossible dream: the perfect centre on the former gasworks. But God had another plan, far more practical than mine. Our house was excellently situated in central Southall, five minutes' walk from the train station. One day in late 2002 a 'For Sale' notice went up outside a nursing home only five doors away from our house. I remember a prayer meeting where Andy McCullough said he felt God was saying that we should look at it. I said 'No!' because it wasn't the perfect centre in the perfect place. However, as usual, Anne was wiser than me and, after some quiet persuasion, we knocked on the door and asked to look around.

The first surprise was that the owners were related to members of St George's, and knew me from services there. They showed us around the building, which consisted of two large, semi-detached houses knocked together. All I can remember from that first visit was the toilets (lots of them – it was a nursing home), beds (fifteen residents), and the smell of stale urine. Yet while by no means 'perfect', it fitted what we needed remarkably well: downstairs bedrooms that could be converted into offices, a large through-lounge with extended dining table, a professionally equipped kitchen, and excellent storage buildings outside. There was also residential accommodation upstairs, and some of the toilets could be converted into showers.

After looking round, we sat down with the owners. I described A Rocha's work and our need for bigger premises. Then we began to talk money. The building was on the market for £642,000. A Rocha had just over £40,000, thanks to an unexpected recent large gift. I swallowed hard, prayed silently, and asked, 'Would you be prepared to take the nursing home off the market for three months to give us a chance to raise the funds?' To me this was a test – we had no hope of buying it without time to raise the money, but why should the owners waste three months, with no guarantees that we could find the cash? After a couple of days, I called the owners. 'Yes,' they said, 'you can have three months, and by the way would you like the industrial-quality cooker, dishwasher, washing machine and fridge as well?'

Now the real test began. With alterations, we probably needed £700,000 altogether – £660,000 more than we already had. Where could we begin? At this point we saw another small piece of God's timing. I mentioned the possibility of the centre in our annual Christmas letter, and one of our friends, Richard Smillie, phoned to see if he could help. We knew Richard's wife Linda better than him – she'd been a vicar in a neighbouring parish. All I knew about Richard's work was that it was something to do with housing. It turned out that he had been chief executive of several housing associations, and knew all there was to know about planning and residential accommodation. I explained that I would be writing to A Rocha UK's supporters, asking if they could do three things. One was obviously to give us money, if they could and wanted to. The second, equally obviously, was to pray that the money would come in. The third was, I thought, a somewhat crazy idea: that perhaps there might be people with money that they didn't need for a while, perhaps saved for retirement, who might give us a fixed-term interest-free loan to help buy the nursing home. Richard sprang into action. With his contacts and experience in housing, he oversaw the legal agreement we needed for this to work, and dealt with all the planning details to do with the purchase. Meanwhile I wrote the big letter, and we all prayed hard as we sent it out.

Each day we waited to see what the post would bring. Sometimes there would be nothing, but often we were humbled and even moved to tears by the letters people sent. It might be a cheque for £10,000, or one for £5 with a note from a pensioner saying this was all they could afford, but that they were praying that, as Jesus had multiplied a few loaves and fishes to feed 5,000 people, so their gift would be multiplied. It took more than three months, but eventually we had gifts from more than 130 different households, and substantial loans from another thirty. When the A Rocha UK board of trustees met in May 2003, the combined total of gifts and loans was £643,513.72 – more than enough to buy the nursing home. The board's minutes simply stated: 'The raising of the funds in such a short time had been a great Christian witness. The chairman led the Board in a prayer of thanksgiving.' With a small loan that Richard Smillie arranged from a Christian housing association for the alterations, we were able to complete the purchase in June 2003. Now we had our centre – not the one I had dreamed of, but clearly the one that God wanted.

By this time the team had grown to ten, so the larger centre was already much needed. Tessa Wilson, Southall born and bred and with parents from the Caribbean, joined us as Finance Officer. Rob and Kathy Thomas came as Centre Managers, once the purchase had been completed, to oversee the transformation of the nursing home into an A Rocha centre. Their arrival was yet another amazing piece in God's jigsaw. Rob was a solicitor with substantial IT experience, and Kathy an NHS laboratory scientist with great artistic skills. When they initially came to see me in 2002, full of enthusiasm after an inspiring visit to A Rocha France, I was at a loss as to how we could use their skills. Then came the centre, and it all fell into place.

One of the great joys of being involved with A Rocha is that it is a genuinely global family, with nationally led projects in nearly twenty countries, and a regular flow of visitors and volunteers. Rob and Kathy, and their successors as centre managers, have provided the welcome and the glue to create a sense of cross-cultural community at the A Rocha UK centre for people from near and far. Over the years we have been joined by team members and volunteers from various parts of the world: Argentina, Austria, Brazil, Czech Republic, France, Georgia, India, Italy, Kenya, Netherlands, New Zealand, Singapore, South Africa, Turkey and the USA, among others. Our locally recruited office team is equally diverse and includes those with Japanese, Punjabi and Grenadian roots. Learning from the cross-cultural wealth of the worldwide Christian church is one of our core values. It challenges the cultural blinkers we are otherwise unaware of, broadening and deepening our experience of God, and also – especially in A Rocha projects – leading to fantastic food!

By the end of 2003, Minet Country Park was open and thriving, we had a good team, and we now had a wonderful new centre for A Rocha UK. However, this was just one project in one local community. The big question was how a vision of our place in God's care for creation could be spread across the UK.

10 The vision expands: A Rocha beyond Southall

I don't think it is enough appreciated how much an outdoor book the Bible is . . . It is best read and understood outdoors, and the farther outdoors the better.[1]
Wendell Berry, Kentucky farmer and essayist

The vision that Anne and I shared was of people in community living out a biblical relationship with God, humanity and nature. What we had first experienced at Cruzinha in Portugal, and struggled to put into practice in urban London, was something that we believed had far wider relevance.

Throughout the UK and far beyond, we could see evidence of a profound dislocation of people from the natural world – in wasteful consuming lifestyles, in an addiction to mobility and speed, and in a complete denial that human welfare is interdependent with the rest of nature on healthy ecosystems. The biggest tragedy was that the Christian church, which should have stood against the tide of individualism and materialism, and in favour of biblical values of community, relationship and dependence, was often no different from the rest of society.

Most of our Christian friends struggled to understand why we were getting so passionate about 'creation care'. Some believed we were simply jumping on the latest secular bandwagon. Others thought that this was a good opportunity for Christians to evangelize the environmental movement. Many struggled to fit our emphasis on conservation and wildlife together with their belief that the gospel was all about people. If A Rocha's work was going to become more than a local backwater in Southall and Hayes, there was clearly a massive job in communication and persuasion to be done.

In discussion with A Rocha UK's trustees, we agreed two main elements in a strategy for A Rocha to become national rather than local. The first was to 'get the message out', and that meant sending me around the country to speak and preach at churches, conferences, festivals, schools, radio stations and anywhere else that would have me.

The second was to seek opportunities for A Rocha-type projects elsewhere in the UK. Because our staffing and finances were so small, there was no way in which we could manage lots of projects, nor did we want to build an A Rocha empire, so our expectation was to grow slowly, and work in partnership with churches and organizations that shared our vision.

* * *

I have always enjoyed speaking and travelling, so I needed little encouragement when invitations began flooding in. I found myself increasingly on the road – rapidly honing my skills in speaking to different audiences, and in producing PowerPoint presentations. I was usually away from home at least three weekends a month, and doing midweek talks as well, sometimes speaking more than twenty times in a month.

Although this meant being away from my family a huge amount (in one year it averaged more than one night in three), both Anne and I felt that the message was so important that this was necessary, and Anne supported me fully. We had a great sense of urgency about alerting people to the huge time bombs of climate change and our over-consuming Western lifestyles, and the fact that the clock is ticking faster. We also felt that there was a great opportunity for moral and spiritual leadership if Christian churches could wake up in time.

From the start I said 'no' to some invitations, and gradually we built up a network of other 'A Rocha speakers' who were trained and resourced to help spread the message, but even so the opportunities kept growing. At the time we had no idea of the long-term impact that my being away so much would eventually have on our family.

I spoke in every corner of Britain, from Aberdeen to Jersey, from Belfast to Kent. One crazy week I spoke on consecutive days in Torquay, Llandudno, Scarborough, Sheffield and London. To begin with, I drove everywhere within the UK. A Rocha UK had been given a hybrid Toyota Prius – at the time the most eco-friendly car available – with an electric engine for urban driving, and a petrol one for long distances. The electric engine was charged through regenerative braking, and by using 'waste' energy from the petrol engine. Although I loved the freedom and thinking time that long-distance driving provides (not to mention the opportunity to stop off at any bird reserves en route), I gradually became convinced that even a hybrid car was not the most environmentally responsible form of travel.

We eventually developed a travel policy at A Rocha whereby we were all encouraged to use public transport when possible. Although I was ethically convinced, I felt like my wings were being clipped, and initially I somewhat begrudged it. However, as with many other sustainable lifestyle changes, I gradually discovered the benefits of using trains. With Britain's overcrowded motorway system leading to frequent hold-ups, trains are often more reliable, and on long journeys much faster. By booking tickets well in advance, and being flexible on timing, I also found train travel to be cheaper than the true cost of running a car.

As A Rocha continued to grow internationally, there were also regular invitations to speak further afield. I had the privilege of speaking right across Europe, from Finland to Portugal, and in Kenya, India and Canada. For international travel there was the genuine dilemma of flying. Although aircraft contribute only 2% of global carbon emissions, air travel is a fast-growing sector, and the altitude at which pollution is released causes it to be more dangerous. It is also one of the areas where ordinary people can make a real difference with their choices.

We took the decision to ban flights within Great Britain, as short-haul flights are proportionately more polluting. When speaking in Europe I would see if train or coach were feasible. When I spoke at a conference in Germany, I enjoyed a stress-free journey by Eurostar and German railways, was able to work while travelling, and discovered that, in both time and cost, there was little difference from flying. At the conference I was shocked to discover that many delegates, who had come from much closer and with excellent rail con-nections, had fallen for the false logic that flying was cheaper and quicker, when with out-of-town airports, check-in times and taxi fares it was neither!

More widely within A Rocha, we try to weigh up the benefits of meeting face-to-face and connecting projects cross-culturally against the true costs of flying. For instance, when A Rocha New Zealand wanted me to take part in a conference, we were able to do the whole thing by Skype, saving money, travel time and the environment. When we do feel that the benefits of flying outweigh the costs, we offset the carbon used through A Rocha's reforest-ation and sustainable-income scheme, Climate Stewards (www.climatestewards.net), but we are careful to emphasize that this is simply some compensation for the environmental damage of flying, rather than an excuse to fly more.

Most of my speaking has been to Christian audiences: talks and seminars at national Christian events such as New Wine, Spring Harvest and Greenbelt, invitations from Bible and theological colleges, and preaching in a great variety of churches from tiny village congregations to massive gatherings in the thousands.

However, the situations I have enjoyed most are those where the audience is not entirely Christian. I have had the enormous privilege of speaking at seminars for the British Ecological Society and for the Darwin Festival, of addressing meetings of national environmental groups such as the British Trust for Conservation Volunteers, Friends of the Earth and the Environment Agency, and of speaking to local wildlife and community groups around the country. Time after time I've found that people resonate and connect with Christianity in a new way once they see it addressing the issues that matter to them. I, and others speaking for A Rocha, have often heard the words: 'If only there were Christians like you around here, I might start going to church.'

As I listened to people's questions, I realized there was a real gap for a book written at a popular level that could communicate the biblical story of God's care for all creation, and our place as creation's caretakers. Eventually I sifted through the material from hundreds of sermons and seminars, and this became the core of my book, *Planetwise: Dare to Care for God's World*.[2]

It has been a huge encouragement for me to find that this has communicated with people so powerfully. The book was kindly endorsed by a wide range of people from the Archbishop of York, John Sentamu, to the environmentalist Jonathan Porritt. It has also been humbling to see how, in some cases, God has used it to change completely people's priorities and lifestyles, not only in the UK, but far beyond.

There have been emails and enquiries about translations from countries as diverse as Pakistan, Brazil, Rwanda and Mongolia. Since *Planetwise* was published in Dutch, I am also now the proud possessor of a book that I've written but cannot understand at all – my daughters would no doubt say that it was translated from Double-Dutch into Dutch!

* * *

As well as speaking and writing, the second major strand in spreading A Rocha's vision was to seek opportunities for further projects. As I spoke, I found that people came alive when I talked about Minet or Portugal, so I realized that what inspires people and influences them to change are the practical stories of creation care. Although solid theology provides essential foundations, people need to see something tangible in order to catch a vision.

Biblically, that's not surprising, for God did not simply send us a book. The Old Testament prophets acted out God's message rather than simply speaking it: often dramatically, as in the case of Ezekiel, who played out the siege of Jerusalem, lying on one side for 390 days (Ezekiel 4); Jeremiah, who bought a field as a sign of hope for the future (Jeremiah 32); and Hosea, whose marriage to the prostitute Gomer became an illustration of human unfaithfulness towards God. When God sent the 'Living Word', Jesus, it was not only to speak but to live out God's message. 'Incarnation', the word for becoming flesh and blood as Jesus did, has always been a fundamental Christian principle, and it is that which makes A Rocha special. It is not simply an organization that campaigns about the environment, but a movement of people and communities committed to living it out in practice.

So if others were to be inspired by seeing Christians caring for creation in a practical way, there needed to be projects within reach of major population areas beyond London.

While we were still in the midst of establishing Minet Country Park, possibilities began to emerge for projects elsewhere. But some would turn out to be more suitable than others. Three wonderful ageing sisters discussed whether their house, with the gardens and fields around it, could be useful for A Rocha. We were attracted by the organic gardening they were doing, and deeply impressed by them as people. However, the house was a Grade 1 listed historic building, which constrained any possibilities of adapting it, and made it hugely expensive to repair and maintain. So, sadly, we said 'no'.

Then came another possibility, this time a house in a wonderful setting on the River Thames, with woods and marshes, and rare plants and birds. It had been left by its former owner to be set up as a conservation trust. We held several meetings with the executors, and our hopes were raised. We even met with A Rocha supporters in the area and involved the local bishop, who was enthusiastic. There was a good rail service to London, and we could see the potential of the site, not only for wildlife, but for bringing groups of children from schools in Southall to 'see the countryside'. That proved to be our undoing, because sadly some of the neighbours in this rather smart Thames-side area apparently did not fancy little urban brats in their neck of the woods. Pressure was put on the executors, and that door closed as well.

* * *

Meanwhile other doors were opening. In North Devon there lies a beautiful Christian retreat and conference centre called Lee Abbey, surrounded by 280 acres of woods, fields and cliffs, all within Exmoor National Park, run by a Christian community of around ninety people, many of them young volunteers from around the world. It is a place of welcome, peace and great natural beauty. It is also one of the most prayer-soaked places I know. Early in the A Rocha UK story, I was invited to speak at a Lee Abbey week on 'Christians in conservation' and I leapt at the chance. Speaking there became a regular annual event, and slowly we realized that we had a lot in common. When Lee Abbey was founded in 1946, part of the original vision had included caring for God's creation.

God's timing is extraordinary, and suddenly all sorts of people began to appear out of Lee Abbey's woodwork, all sharing a vision of creation and community working together. Eventually a formal partnership was agreed, whereby the management of both the estate and the house would undergo a complete environmental review and A Rocha-linked conferences would happen regularly there. The partnership continues to grow and develop, with Lee Abbey researching its own on-site green energy production via a small hydro-electric plant, and a continuing programme of educating community and guests about creation care and sustainable living.

Lee Abbey is unique, but there are many Christian conference centres, colleges, schools, retreat centres and even private estates, with land which is of real ecological importance. Just as God sent Adam to 'tend and keep' the garden of creation, Christian individuals and organizations today are entrusted with serving and preserving the areas God has entrusted to them. It would be wonderful to see a whole range of places inspired by this vision. To look after the land well, to value it, protect it, and enhance it for wildlife is a Christian responsibility, and a witness to God as Creator and Redeemer.

* * *

Of course most of us do not live on or own great estates. In Britain most of us now live in towns and cities where we often see the environment damaged by carelessness and neglect.

We may complain about it, but do we ever try to do anything about it? Norman Crowson does.

I first met Norman a couple of years into working with A Rocha. He has a broad northern accent, having lived and worked in the Derbyshire-Yorkshire borders all his life. Though retired from lecturing in engineering, he is one of the most energetic people I know. Until his late sixties he was a canoeing instructor, taking outward-bound courses. He's also a proficient wildlife photographer, a keen bird-watcher, and he's deeply involved in his local Baptist church. When Norman first said, 'Dave, I'd like you to come up and visit me – I've got some ideas', I mumbled something about being too busy, but I've come to learn that Norman rarely takes 'no' for an answer.

Eventually Norman got me up to Dronfield, between Sheffield and Chesterfield, chiefly, if unfairly, famous for 'the Dronfield bypass', an accident black-spot of elevated dual-carriageway that carries the A61 past the town. After I preached at his church, Norman told me of his great plan.

He'd started a small A Rocha local group at the Baptist church. They held 'bird-and-flower' walks into the Derbyshire Dales, to which people from other churches came as well. Next they planned a series of Bible studies, based around Bishop James Jones' book *Jesus and the Earth*. This was just the beginning. Norman wanted to put on a 'green fair' at the church and invite all the regional environmental groups, ranging from the RSPB, Chesterfield Council and Friends of the Earth, to the North East Derbyshire Badger Group, and of course A Rocha. He asked if I would come up to speak at a special evening on 'Believing in conservation', showing how what we believe affects how we treat nature, followed by a question-and-answer panel. Finally, on the Sunday morning, would I preach at a conservation-themed guest service at his church?

Norman clearly had a vision, both to care for creation and to use this as a way of getting Christian and non-Christian together. I was hooked, and booked. It was thrilling to be engaging with the important questions people ask, not in a confrontational way, but as fellow environmentalists who are passionate and want to see things improve.

Norman still hadn't finished. He told me that Dronfield and District Council of Churches, seventeen local congregations from across the denominational spectrum, were planning a week of mission the following year to be led by the evangelist Rob Frost.[3] I had worked closely with Rob, a man with a heart for Jesus who had become convinced that creation care is not an optional extra, but integral to Christian mission. Rob used to say, 'When Christians take the earth seriously, people take the gospel seriously', and insisted that there be a practical environmental aspect to every mission that his team conducted.

Norman was asked if he would organize an environmental project as part of the mission. Running through the centre of Dronfield is the Lea Brook Valley, a typical semi-urban watercourse which had been neglected over the years. It had litter and fly-tipping, overgrown brambles and blockages in the stream. Why not use the mission as an opportunity to get Lea Brook cleaned up and improved for wildlife and local people? Then the local churches could commit to 'tending and keeping it' long term. This was a wonderful vision and, with Norman's drive, local contacts, and input from others in A Rocha UK, it came to fruition.

Students from the Methodist College at Cliff in Derbyshire joined with Rob Frost's team and local Christians from across Dronfield to transform the valley, with the full support of the town council as landowners, and of local conservation groups. In fact the council, which had previously not had a particularly positive relationship with local churches, was delighted, even supplying equipment and risk assessments. Workers cleared skip-loads of rubbish, replaced ugly graffiti with attractive murals, built board-walks and bridges, erected bird and bat boxes, and, in short, the valley was transformed. As litter-pickers from local churches walked through the valley, they stopped and prayed. Today the project continues to develop, and volunteers from local churches patrol and manage the valley.

Not many of us may have the energy of Norman but, perhaps on a less ambitious scale, what has happened in Dronfield could well serve as a model for further projects around the UK. In almost every community there are places that are neglected and uncared for. If Christians are not only to speak about, but to *be* good news for their communities, then what more tangible way of demonstrating it? Moreover, in a time of environmental fear, what better way of showing that there is hope: that we need to start making a difference where we live?

* * *

As the M40 motorway snakes between London and Oxford, it slices through a cutting in the Chiltern Hills, next to the village of Lewknor, right by Junction 6. The ancient village church appears briefly at the start of each episode of the popular television series *The Vicar of Dibley*. One day the vicar of Lewknor and its surrounding villages, Simon Brignall, contacted me out of the blue with an idea for a new project.

Lewknor sits strategically not just beside the M40, but near the Ridgeway National Trail. Above it is Aston Rowant National Nature Reserve, a beautiful area managed by Natural England for its rare flowers and butterflies.

Lewknor is also in the middle of the area where the majestic red kite has been successfully reintroduced. These aerial acrobats, soaring effortlessly on air-currents and eddies, have come to symbolize the area. In medieval times they were common urban birds, flocking above meat and fish markets, but later were relentlessly persecuted and became extinct in England. Then in 1989, the RSPB and the Nature Conservancy Council began a reintroduction scheme in the Chilterns, using birds from healthy European populations. Red kites quickly re-established themselves, and this has been so successful that the population has been used for further reintroductions around the UK.

Simon Brignall had noticed that many people were visiting the area to see red kites, to look for other wildlife and rare flowers at Aston Rowant, or simply to enjoy walking in the Chilterns. Yet there were no facilities for visitors or school groups, and conversations with Natural England and other bodies suggested they were keen for a visitors' centre. What if the ancient parish church in Lewknor could become not only home to a worshipping community, but a place of welcome and information for visitors and schoolchildren? What if, through A Rocha, there was also a clear link between the environmental message and the Christian faith that the building represented?

Like all visions, it has taken a long time, hard work, and many compromises in the journey from idea to reality. Simon has moved on to another parish, and funding for a part-time education worker has proved hard to sustain. However, increasing voluntary involvement from Christians in local villages, partnerships with Natural England and the local church primary school, and a series of imaginative community events, have led to a thriving locally managed project. Events have included displays and special services in the church, working parties and community events at Aston Rowant, and a farmers' market in the churchyard celebrating sustainably produced local food. If Living Water-ways provided an inspiration for urban initiatives around the UK, Chiltern Gateway has shown what can happen in a rural area too.

* * *

From the launch of A Rocha UK, I was seriously overworking. In the early years, the Living Waterways project alone was a full-time job, and on top of that, the national vision meant weekends travelling around the country. It was clear that I could not carry on indefinitely at that pace. My daughters were growing fast, and all too often I would miss special performances at school or sometimes even their birthdays. Anne and I were keen that they should grow up sharing both our Christian faith and our environmental values, so we didn't want them resenting their dad's work.

Of course the growing team shared the load in terms of administration and finance, yet a team needed managing. While those who were joining the team were committed and capable, most were also relatively young and inexperienced in leadership. From as early as 2002, I asked the trustees for help in managing the team and the projects as they grew. The difficulty, as ever with small growing organizations, was finding the right people, and the money to pay them.

Then Pete Hawkins turned up. He first emailed from Australia, where he'd been travelling with his family, and mentioned that, while in Canada, he'd encountered A Rocha and was keen to get involved. Previously Pete had been running a small Christian consultancy, helping other charities, mainly Christian social-work organizations, develop and grow their capacity. He'd been doing this single-handed for some years and, while on sabbatical, felt God provoking him in a new direction, as he became increasingly concerned about environmental and lifestyle issues.

Pete and I walked around Minet Country Park, gently sounding each other out. It was soon clear that we were like chalk and cheese. I have always been an enthusiast, an ideas person, something of a visionary, with a passion for communication. Pete was a careful, steady organizer, with a concern for process and structure. Both of us were strategic thinkers, but whereas I could see where A Rocha UK could be in ten years' time and wanted to inspire people with the vision, Pete could immediately see the difficulties in the way, and the steps we would need to take to overcome them. While I kept spouting hot air, Pete knew how to construct a balloon to harness the energy into something productive!

It was obvious to me that Pete was God's man for A Rocha UK, with abilities that complemented mine. Amazingly, and he deliberately revealed this only after we'd agreed in principle to work together, he came complete with his own funding. He had been raising his own support in his previous role, from friends and churches, and was hopeful that his supporters would believe in this new vision sufficiently to continue supporting him in finance and prayer.

It was clearly going to be a challenging relationship. If there were two sides to an issue, Pete and I would inevitably take them to start with, and it would be hard-headed discussion (on my part), and gentle determined persuasion (on Pete's), before we eventually met somewhere in the middle. Besides all that, I (along with various other people in A Rocha) was a keen bird-watcher, and Pete wasn't particularly. At one infamous meeting, he was carefully explaining something when somebody pointed out the window, and suddenly everybody else around the table disappeared to look at a soaring buzzard, leaving Pete understandably perplexed.

Pete and I also experienced the pain of transition from initiating to establishing an organization, handing over control of something that had previously been your vision and passion, for which you have sacrificed your best years, especially when you know that there will inevitably be changes of direction and emphasis that you will find difficult. It is equally hard to be, as Pete has been, the person in the background who comes in and steadily builds a solid organization, nurtures good relationships, ensures strategic development, and yet rarely gets the same credit as the pioneering leader.

I am attempting to be honest about differences and difficulties. Too many Christian books gloss over painful relationships and unanswered questions. Yet my experience in A Rocha and elsewhere is that not only are these the norm, but that it is in persevering through difficulties that we often see God at work most powerfully. In 2 Corinthians 4, Paul uses an image of the Christian as a clay vessel, not a perfect porcelain heirloom but a rough-and-ready everyday utensil with imperfections and fragilities. It is because we are so ordinary, so unremarkable, that the light of Christ's transforming love can be seen more clearly shining through us. Sadly we spend our time trying to hide the flaws, polish our common clay pots, and pretend they are bone china, falsely thinking that people will be impressed either with us, or with what God has made out of us.

In our life with A Rocha, struggling to live in community and to get on with people of very different personalities and cultures, it has often been impossible to hide the truth even if we have wanted to. It's what Miranda Harris, co-founder of A Rocha, has called 'living life inside-out', when all the hidden attitudes and secret habits get revealed in the pressures of community living. Yet we find, time and again, that Paul's picture is right. Somehow, visitors and volunteers learn to see through our mistakes and flaws, and glimpse something rather special beyond: the light of Christ.

Over the years I have gradually learned to value, and work with, people who are very different from me. Through it all – to change the image from clay vessels to uncut gemstones – I have observed how God uses the tidal churning of uncomfortable relationships and the sharp laser of painful self-awareness slowly to change us into the people he wants us to be.

As A Rocha UK grew, Pete and I were joined by others in a slowly evolving management team. Richard Smillie, who had advised us on the purchase of the A Rocha Centre, came on board longer term as part-time Managing Director in 2003–2006, looking after many aspects of A Rocha's development.

Then, in the summer of 2005, CMS (who were already supporting Anne and me as mission partners seconded to A Rocha) mentioned that they had somebody who was interested in working with A Rocha UK. Sian Hawkins turned out to be an amazing woman who had managed community projects in Afghanistan with CMS for some years, and spoke Dari, but also had a first degree in environmental science. Encouraged by others, I had made the hard decision that I could not continue combining my increasingly busy national role with trying to lead the Living Waterways project in Southall and Hayes. Sian was perfectly gifted to become Director of A Rocha Living Waterways.

But the transition was never going to be easy for either of us. Sian had the founder and former Director still working in the same team, and finding it hard not to interfere with the project he had now handed over. I meanwhile found it agonizing to let go of 'my baby', and to accept that others would take the project in new directions. Both of us could fight our corner, but we were also mature enough to recognize our weaknesses, and often one or both would have to calm down and apologize. It helped greatly that Sian and Anne became close friends – and Anne was often able to defuse tensions or help me see things from Sian's point of view. Eventually we developed a mutual respect, and when Sian eventually moved on to pursue further studies, she left a huge gap in our team and our lives.

When Richard Smillie moved on in 2006, we desperately needed somebody else with leadership experience to oversee A Rocha UK's growth. As before, God's timing was perfect. In late 2005, I received an email from Steve Hughes, a student at London School of Theology, asking to do a term-time placement. Initially I didn't reply, partly because I knew that short-term placements could simply mean extra work in supervision. Steve persisted and I agreed to meet him. I had been picturing a twenty-something student with little life experience, so I was somewhat surprised to encounter a mature man in his mid-fifties.

It turned out that Steve had taken early retirement after more than thirty years with Shell, where he had risen to become a Senior Vice-President for Human Resources. He was doing a year's theology course while seeking God's leading for the next stage of his life and, as a keen naturalist, wanted to look at A Rocha, particularly to understand the theology of caring for creation. Over the next few months Steve's placement consisted largely of long conversations about the Bible and the environment, while he chauffeured me to speaking engagements. Halfway through the placement, Steve offered to give three days a week to A Rocha, 'if we could use him'.

If we could use him, indeed! Until this point I'd been reluctant to let go of the overall vision and direction of A Rocha UK, but Steve brought a wonderful combination of experience, wisdom, gentleness and vision. He was appointed Chief Executive Officer, and became a trusted leader for the whole team.

Under Steve's leadership, A Rocha UK has grown into a truly national organization, with a team that has now grown to more than forty (many of them part-time volunteers). Pete Hawkins has helped transform the internal culture, overseeing changes in strategy, branding, marketing, communications and good management practice, as well as implementing a regional structure. Sian Hawkins consolidated team relationships, and put Living Waterways on a more professional footing. With Andy Lester, A Rocha UK's conservation strategy has developed, with the capacity to offer paid consultancy to Christian organizations and a system of Associated Projects which sign up to A Rocha UK's values and standards, but are locally managed and financed.

Most importantly, the board has approved a 'movement strategy', clarifying A Rocha's vision as not seeking to run lots of centrally managed projects, but rather inspiring and resourcing the growing number of 'A Rocha Friends' in living out the values wherever they are. That meant not only encouraging practical, locally run projects, but also looking at the thorny and uncomfortable issue of our 'lifestyles'.

11 Lessons in lifestyle

*Always bear in mind that very little indeed is necessary for living
a happy life.*[1]
Emperor Marcus Aurelius

*Affluenza: n. a painful, contagious, virally transmitted condition
of overload, debt, anxiety, and waste resulting from the dogged
pursuit of more.*[2]
John De Graaf

It took many years from the experience in the Isles of Scilly
with which I began this book, until Anne and I started
working through the implications for our own lifestyles. This
is not unusual. It's one thing to be persuaded intellectually
that caring for God's creation is integral to Christian faith.
It is quite another for that theoretical belief to affect your
daily lifestyle choices. This parallels many people's journey
to faith – a development from 'belonging' to 'believing' to
'behaving'. Many people get to know Christians first, then
become persuaded of the Christian message, but only very
gradually does it affect their relationships, finances, politics
and other lifestyle areas. Behaviour is always last.

As we looked at our own lives, we could see the same disconnection between what we were saying and what we were

doing. What was the sense in my travelling so much, when I was preaching about the biblical value of rootedness in a particular place and community? Where was consistency if we were so busy working for A Rocha and juggling a growing family that most of our meals were ready-packed instant supermarket food?

The more that Anne and I reflected, the more we were challenged to change how we lived day to day. Our first step, well before the days of A Rocha UK, was to use washable, reusable nappies when Hannah, our first child, was born. We weighed up the cost of buying them against the annual cost of disposables, and realized that (even with washing factored in) we would save a small fortune. In fact we saved even more, as we discovered that they lasted so well that they could be passed on from child to child, including being lent out to others when we were between children. Our record was five or six children in turn using the same nappies, before they eventually deteriorated. The extra washing and drying were hard work – especially for Anne – so we tried not to be too Pharisaical and allowed ourselves to use disposables on holiday or overnight.

When Hannah started attending school, she challenged us about driving her to school. She must have been about five when she said, 'Don't drive, daddy. It makes the puddles dirty!' The journey was only half a mile, but I always had an excuse – either it was raining or I was in a hurry to get back for something. It had to be a conscious decision, going against the grain of my comfortable rushed life, that it was actually better to walk. Soon I discovered that it really was better. The walk to school became one of the highlights of the day, in terms of quality time with the children: listening to their excited chatter or minor worries, and sometimes making up stories as we went along. I realized we were walking past other parents getting into their cars for the same journey, and yet, partly because of a one-way system and partly because of traffic congestion, we would often get to the school before them, and never became caught up in the chaos of everybody leaving the school gates at once.

Slowing down, having time to look and listen, changed my relationship with the local area. I became more aware of the rubbish on the streets, which houses were cared for, and which had processions of temporary lodgers. I also became more sensitive to the social and spiritual atmosphere of Southall. Anne sometimes used to 'prayer walk' with the children on the way to school. Our third daughter Rosie, when she was in nursery, put her own twist on this by saying, 'Mummy, can we pray for that house – the one with the blue door?' or 'That one – No. 39?' Eventually Anne realized there was a pattern to Rosie's childlike praying, and that the same house kept coming up day after day. She began quietly praying for whoever lived there.

Months later, as she sat watching the children in the playground of the local park, she got into conversation with an Asian Muslim mother who was clearly upset. This lady opened up (as people do with Anne), and shared her many troubles, relieved to find somebody she could talk to. Anne offered to pray for her and, as they parted, asked where she lived. Out of the thousands of houses in Southall, it was one of those that little Rosie kept asking her to pray for, and Anne was able to share that she'd already been praying for this lady for months. For us it was a reminder that the simple clear faith of children has a power and perceptiveness – a sensitivity to God's Spirit – that adults are often closed to. It was also a reminder that nothing is wasted, however trivial it seems, if it is offered to God. Even something as small as walking rather than driving to the school or shops, or just prayerfully 'loitering with intent' around your local area, can be powerfully used in God's purposes.

On another occasion our second daughter, Rebekah, was travelling with her sisters and mother on a train, and became annoyed at all the litter in the carriage. She started picking it up, and soon filled a plastic bag. As there was so much more, she asked other passengers if they had empty bags she could use. Before long, whether by inspiring or shaming them, she had everybody in the carriage helping her and talking to one another, as people emerged from behind their newspapers and MP3 players to join in cleaning the train. I don't want to pretend that our children are all angels or fanatical eco-warriors, but there is something special about the way children see things so clearly, and refuse to compromise with what's wrong. Certainly Anne and I have often been challenged by our children to follow through the principles that we've tried to teach them.

All of these were simply first steps in a gradual overhaul of our whole lifestyles, which is still ongoing. We certainly do not wish to hold ourselves up as any kind of model 'green family', both because we know how many compromises we still make, and because we have friends who have gone much further than us. However, whenever I spoke for A Rocha and shared our lifestyle journey, I found others seeking to do something similar. Particularly within A Rocha there were many people seeking to live out biblical values of simpler sustainable living wherever they were.

I had been especially challenged by meditating on Psalm 24:1, which simply reminds us that 'The earth is the LORD's and everything in it'. What if that assertion, that it is God's world not ours, really filtered through to our lifestyle choices? What if our shopping, our travel, our attitudes to money and possessions really reflected God's ownership of creation?

Gradually the idea began to form for a 'lifestyle pledge' that reflected biblical values of simplicity, sustainability and community, helping people to take small, simple, progressive steps to transform their lifestyles. After consulting with others, we decided to name the scheme 'Living Lightly 24-1', linking to Psalm 24:1 and to the fact that a lifestyle journey is about twenty-four-hour-a-day discipleship. We also wanted it to be 'lightly' not simply in lessening our ecological footprint, but in rediscovering a lightness of touch, a lack of care and worry about our material security stemming from a deeper trust in God.

Soon after launching 'Living Lightly 24-1', Anne and I were asked to speak at the New Wine Christian summer festival. I had done seminars at New Wine several times before, and had noticed a steady growth in the number of Christians attending who were concerned about the environment. However, the seminars had still not touched the vast majority of people. This time it was different. We were asked to speak on 'Living lightly', were given the largest venue, and also broadcast on New Wine Radio. Hundreds of people came along as we shared about our struggles as a family to live more sustainably, and about God's heart for us to be free of materialism. Anne even brought baskets of vegetables from her allotment to show and give away.

Afterwards we were surrounded by dozens of people with questions, and the A Rocha stand was swamped with people signing up to 'Living Lightly 24-1'. It was as if, after digging for water in an environmental desert, we had suddenly struck a powerful underground river. Most of those present were like us, busy, working families deeply discontented with the values of a stressful, selfish, materialist culture, struggling to live out biblical values, and desperate to be part of a wider movement to support them.

Living Lightly 24-1 has continued to develop under Ruth Valerio's management. Ruth had been on a parallel lifestyle journey herself, and was perfectly placed to develop the scheme as she joined A Rocha UK part-time. Some of her own story is found in her excellent book 'L' is for Lifestyle, which goes through an A–Z of ethical lifestyle issues, one of those few books that manages to be both challenging and encouraging at the same time. The scheme is now simply known as 'Living Lightly', and has a growing number of people committed to moving step-by-step towards simpler living.

Meanwhile the Bookless Bunch were finding that our lifestyle journey sometimes pushed us further than we'd intended. In August 2007, driving down to stay with friends in Cornwall, with four children, bicycles and masses of luggage on board, I came over a blind summit in Somerset suddenly to find a queue of traffic. I managed to stop, but the car behind crashed sickeningly into our rear end. The children were shaken but not injured, the boot sported a huge dent with the bike-carrier mangled into it, yet amazingly the car appeared safe to drive. We limped down to Cornwall, but when the insurance assessors looked at our car, the news was bad. I'm still not sure if 'beyond economical repair' really means a car needs to be junked or is just a symptom of society's urge to replace rather than repair, but we had no choice. The insurance company provided a replacement car for the holiday and to get us home, and then we were faced with a difficult choice.

The fact was that my big mouth had landed us in it! I had often spoken about how we need to break our addiction to driving and look at lower-carbon ways of travelling. I knew all about the various electric, hybrid and fuel-efficient models available, and had publicly said that, when our large family car wore out, we would look hard at living without one. So we didn't really have a choice! We decided that we would try to live for three months without a car and see how we got on. After all, we reasoned, London has excellent public transport.

It was tough. Shopping for six people without a vehicle meant a lot of heavy bags on the bus. The girls also now had clubs and activities after school, and friends to meet up with at weekends. We were happy with our eldest taking the bus by herself, but not after dark, and, as the nights drew in, we realized that the children's safety was a major argument for having a vehicle.

It so happens that Southall is not only a wonderful multiracial cauldron of cultures and foods, it is also home to the UK's sole supplier of the Reva G-Wiz: a funky little all-electric vehicle designed in California and made in Bangalore. We'd seen them around and, after taking a test drive, fell in love with them. Soon we took possession of a second-hand glorified dodgem car, maximum speed forty miles per hour, maximum journey before recharging forty miles (as long as wipers or lights weren't needed), two comfortable adult seats in the front and two small child-size seats in the back. It charged via an ordinary electric socket, so initially we had the lead going through our letter-box before fitting an external charging-point on the house. The cost of electricity (even on our one-hundred-per-cent-green tariff from Good Energy) was two to three pence per mile compared with fifteen to twenty pence for a petrol car.

An electric car isn't the solution for everybody, but in our urban setting it was perfect. It would carry our shopping, take kids to and from friends' houses, even transport bird-ringing equipment to Minet. On most of the occasions when all six of us were travelling together, it was either local enough to use public transport, or we could book ahead and get train tickets. We reckoned that we would need to hire a larger vehicle only a few times each year, such as for holidays, and that over the year we would actually save money as well as being greener. In the end, we haven't needed to hire a vehicle, as some good A Rocha friends loaned us their car while work took them to Australia for a few years. We use this as a last resort, usually taking the electric car, public transport and, as the kids have got older, often all cycling together to church, the swimming pool or to local events.

In *Planetwise* I wrote about how neither of us had any gardening experience but we gradually began to grow a few herbs and salad leaves in the garden, before Anne took the big step of renting an allotment. It was very much her project, with my encouragement and occasional unskilled labour. I have waxed lyrical about the goodness of vegetables and salad that we have grown ourselves, without food miles, pesticides or preservatives, which taste intensely and wonderfully fresh. I've also talked about how our children became more positive about eating their greens when they'd helped to grow them, and of how Anne's relationship with God was deepened as she followed the cycle of weeding, planting, watering and waiting for fruitfulness, and turned this into prayer for herself and others.

What I probably haven't written enough about is the sheer hard work and struggles that have gone alongside this. An allotment is effectively a small market garden, and like any farming it demands a huge amount of work, often at unsocial hours. In the summer, Anne would be down there almost every evening, watering and weeding, and it sometimes felt as if we hardly saw each other any more. She had a constant battle against invasive weeds, in our case the virulent mare's tail, a plant that apparently survived the extinction of the dinosaurs and seemed determined to see us off too. If you pulled it up, it sprouted again from every hair-thin tendril. If we went away on holiday, it would cover the whole patch by the time we returned. One winter, Anne put thick plastic sheeting across a large area to try to kill it off, but when she removed it months later she found a thick carpet of mare's tail laughing at her efforts.

Some time later we found ourselves on a conference held at Windsor Castle with a range of the world's top environmental experts. We asked advice about mare's tail from Sir Ghillean Prance. His response was clear: the only ways to get rid of it were either to leave the whole area covered in thick plastic for five years, or to use a commercial herbicide.

Our organic idealism had run into the realities of a fallen world, of the battle against weeds and thorns that people have faced since Adam and Eve left Eden. We had always known that growing our own food wouldn't be easy, but the reality was still much harder than we'd expected. Perhaps we were simply too urbanized, so used to finding instantly all we wanted on the shelves of supermarkets, that the setbacks of an allotment were too much for us.

Some people would have given up at this point, but not Anne. When increasingly dry summers meant that most crops failed, she proposed growing olives and figs. When an accident after slipping on ice meant that her knee ligaments were badly injured and recovery took over a year, she plodded on. Even when the children gradually lost interest and her husband complained she was never at home, she kept bringing back delicious tomatoes, rainbow chard and leeks. Not even the mare's tail could put her off. She decided to split the allotment, carefully treating one half with herbicide while she farmed the other half, and then switching over. The particular herbicide is designed to bond with the weed and then break down into organic components, leaving no harmful residue in the soil for other plants, so she was happy about growing food afterwards.

I have gone into some detail here because there are so many simplistic and romantic stories about 'going green'. They downplay the fact that there is much about it that is simply hard slog: going against the grain of our culture and sometimes going against the grain of a rebellious fallen nature. Some environmentalists talk idealistically about the earth as if all we need to do is attune ourselves more closely to nature and everything will be fine. Of course there's an element of truth in this: God does want us to be aware of our connection with the soil from which he formed us ('Adam' from *adamah*). We are far more likely to live sustainably if we are aware of our interdependence on natural systems, as were the psalmists and prophets, and as Jesus encouraged us to be in the Sermon on the Mount. However, the Bible is equally clear that we are no longer in the Garden of Eden. Nature is not only beautiful and full of God's sustaining presence; it also has elements that are wild and dangerous and need bringing under control. It is in this context that we need to see God's charge to humanity in Genesis 1 to 'rule over' and 'subdue' an unruly creation. Like Anne with the mare's tail, there are times when we need to act, if we are to make the garden more fruitful overall.

Our discussions as a family about eating meat were another example of the dilemmas of living in a fallen world. In 2004–2005 we had the enormous privilege as a whole family of spending two months travelling around India by train, combining A Rocha engagements with visiting my childhood haunts, seeing families of Southall friends, and watching wildlife. Naomi-Ruth was three, and for the first time she made the connection between animals and meat. We'd been staying in Mizoram in the far north east of India, and it was Christmas time. Mizoram is overwhelmingly Christian, and every household seemed to have a pig that was being fattened for the Christmas feast. One evening there was the sound of horrific squealing all around the town, and rivulets of blood in the streets, and the next day we were offered pork to eat. This was too much for Naomi-Ruth. 'I don't want to eat anything which has had a face on it' was our three-year-old's statement of vegetarian principle.

For Rebekah, our second daughter, meat had already become quite an issue. She has always been both remarkably sensitive and totally determined. One day, aged five, she had asked, 'Do you have to be a Hindu to be a vegetarian?' Her best friends at school were Hindus, and they were the only vegetarians she knew. She had independently concluded that animals had to die for us to eat meat, and her sense of justice was appalled. We agreed that, if she still felt the same by her seventh birthday, she could go vegetarian. Being Rebekah, she remembered, and rather than cooking two dishes for every meal, Anne and I decided we would all move to a more vegetarian diet, with an alternative for Rebekah when we ate meat. She had provoked us to think through issues of animal welfare from a Christian viewpoint, and the more I researched it the more shocked I was, both at the mistreatment of animals in intensive farming practices and at the silence of the Christian church, when the Bible is full of injunctions about respecting and caring for all living things.

Some time after this we were visiting some farming friends for lunch, and had failed to warn them about our veggie daughter. As they served roast pork, Rebekah caught Anne's eye and made a face. With an inspired thought, Anne spoke to our hosts: 'Rebekah's usually vegetarian, but could you tell us the story of where this pork came from?' They caught on and explained how the pig had been reared on their neighbour's farm, fed and treated well, given access to the outdoors and space to mix with other pigs, and how at the end they had killed it quickly and humanely, and were thankful to God for the gift of good meat to eat. 'I'd like to try some please,' was Rebekah's response. 'It's had a happy life and that's what matters.'

'Only eat happy meat,' became our family motto. We have reduced our meat eating as a family yet further, partly because methane emissions from cattle, and tropical deforestation to create ranches, are major contributors to global warming. We now eat meat only once or twice a week and when we do we ensure that it is organic or at least free-range, and as locally produced as possible. For us this has become an essential part of following Jesus. If all things in creation are made 'by him and for him' (Colossians 1:16), if

God notices when a single sparrow falls to the ground, if God cares that farm animals get a good rest on the Sabbath, then animal welfare is not an optional extra for Christians.

We found that our family's lifestyle decisions sometimes clashed with the values of friends or A Rocha colleagues. When we had discussions on food policy as a team, it sometimes seemed to me, with my tendency to want everything black or white, that the desire to get cheap food was more powerful than the moral case to treat God's creation with respect. I have had to accept that you cannot force people to change their lifestyles. However frustratingly slow it is, people have to come to their own conclusions. Gradually A Rocha's food policy has evolved to take note of animal welfare, and to realize that God's call on us to 'rule over' the birds and animals is not a licence to exploit, but an invitation to share God's loving care for creation.

At the same time as being honest about the struggles of going green, the last thing I want to do is put people off! We live on a small planet with finite resources, and a population that is forecast to reach ten billion by 2050. In Western countries we have swallowed the lie that prosperity can continue for ever, that growth is unlimited and nobody suffers. In fact, as Bishop James Jones and Sir John Houghton have powerfully put it, 'We live in times when we are raping the Earth and exploiting the poor.'[3] In the West, where all of us are part of the world's richest 20%, we consume sixteen times as much of the earth's resources as the world's poorest 20%. Nor is it a simple matter of letting the poor 'catch up'. The painful truth is that if everybody had a lifestyle like the average Briton, we would need three earth-sized planets to provide the resources.

So we have to change: to simplify our lives and reduce our ecological impact. We have to do it rapidly because of the imminent threat of runaway climate change, and also because of the global deforestation, wildlife extinction, pollution and waste that our lifestyles are causing. We also have to change rapidly because the world's poor are becoming poorer, as a direct result of the injustices of world trade, and as an indirect result of the environmental changes that our lifestyles cause.

Yet it is not all negative. Despite the urgency of the crisis, and the difficulty of going against our materialistic culture, there is also good news in living more simply. Sociologists and others have written of the epidemic of 'affluenza' sweeping Western nations. This has been defined as 'a painful, contagious, virally transmitted condition of overload, debt, anxiety, and waste resulting from the dogged pursuit of more'.[4] Reducing our addiction to filling the inner void with 'retail therapy' or electronic games, to travelling faster and further, to earning more yet enjoying less, can only be good for us. Reconnecting with nature and our place in it, rediscovering that 'being' is more important than 'doing', that genuine relationships give more satisfaction than inanimate or virtual ones: all these have great social, psychological and physical benefits. Putting down deeper roots in the places where God has planted us, learning to live by the rhythms of God's creation, discovering God's whisper in the wind blowing through trees, or feeling his power in a green stem pushing its way through the cold soil, can all be ways in which our souls are renewed and our relationship with God is deepened. It is not just for the sake of the planet and the poor that we need to live lightly. It is for our own sakes and, most of all, for the sake of the God who longs for us to stop running, and to rest in his presence.

12 Coming home

God is involved in 'building to last', in creating a sustainable world
and sustainable relationships with us human beings. He doesn't
give up on the material of human lives. He doesn't throw it all away
and start again. And he asks us to approach one another and our
physical world with the same commitment. The life of Jesus, the
life in which God identifies completely with our flesh and blood,
is the supreme sign of that commitment. God doesn't do waste.[1]
Archbishop Rowan Williams

Heaven is important, but it's not the end of the world.[2]
Bishop N. T. Wright

At the end of 2008, I looked back at how A Rocha UK had
grown and changed since its launch eight years previously.
I reflected in my article how

> the tiny seed of an idea has snowballed into an ever-growing
> and ever-accelerating national movement. There is simply so
> much going on now! The team has grown so fast, the projects,
> partnerships and potential for further growth seem limitless.
> In recent years my own diary has filled up before I've even
> opened it with requests for talks, conferences, articles and
> advice – and I've had to work hard to protect precious time off.[3]

I then wrote about the pain of handing over leadership to others, of letting go of 'our babies' in terms of the Living Waterways project and the vision for how A Rocha UK would develop. I admitted that saying 'yes' to so many requests to speak and travel had partly become my way of escaping from the changes that were inevitably taking place. Of course that wasn't the only reason I was away so much. There was a genuine growth in significant speaking opportunities to cathedrals, colleges and conferences, and these were invitations that Anne, the trustees and the management team agreed I had to take. It was also easier for my colleagues if I wasn't always around breathing down their necks. Yet it was clear that there was a growing disconnection between my itinerant life and my growing family.

In the article I continued:

> There have been warning signs I should have heeded earlier:
> missing important milestones in my children's lives, events
> at our church, and rare birds on Minet (!) . . . or being in the
> A Rocha Centre in Southall one lunch-time when a local
> volunteer who had been helping for several weeks turned
> and said to me: 'And are you visiting for the first time?'

Most importantly, while I was away so much, it was obvious that Anne was struggling more and more. She had recognized over the previous couple of years that she was gradually sinking into depression. The causes were many and complex – in fact it's true to say we still haven't disentangled all of them, and maybe never will. It's also not appropriate to go into all of them here.

One cause, and only one amongst several, was the fact that Anne had become increasingly marginal as A Rocha UK had grown. We had founded it together, been joint team leaders, and shared the vision, planning, prayer and sacrifice. It was a joint calling. Yet as A Rocha grew, Anne found herself more and more on the edge. She continued to work part-time, focusing on managing the UK website, but no longer attending key meetings where vision was shared and decisions were made. It's important to say that we don't blame anybody for this – there was no conscious attempt to shut Anne out – it was simply a consequence of A Rocha UK becoming more professional, and Anne's visionary role not being clearly defined. Whereas I was becoming nationally known for my speaking and writing, Anne was being left in the shadows – the forgotten co-founder of A Rocha UK.

Through 2007 and 2008, Anne went weekly to see a Christian counsellor, which helped enormously in understanding and facing her past and present issues. But her mental health continued to decline, and by the autumn of 2008 she was on anti-depressants and under the care of a psychiatrist. In the Christmas letter to our friends, she wrote about her state of mind:

> I sit in my dressing gown, typing on my shiny purple laptop, the fog of sedation briefly clearing enough to open up a window of clear thought. The confident multitasking Anne, who could juggle her roles as wife, mother and friend whilst doing pioneer work setting up A Rocha Living Waterways, now finds herself unable to focus on even the simplest task of cooking a meal for the family – in the past fortnight has left the gas ring on unlit, burnt food into pans, left food uneaten in the microwave, gone to do the washing-up and found I'd already done it (there have to be some perks to losing my mind!), the list goes on . . .
>
> What has this meant for the rest of the family? Whenever I do something strange, there is a cheeky chorus from the girls, 'Mum, how many tablets have you taken today?!' They seem to have understood well that I am depressed but I am not at risk, and seem secure in the knowledge that things will get better. Dave carries the deepest burden of anxiety about

my current state of mind, and whilst we both see this as something I will come out of (hopefully sooner rather than later!), he feels the heavy weight of responsibility for making sure that the family functions – that the children still get to school, the shopping and washing get done, and all of this whilst working hard on A Rocha UK responsibilities.

Early in 2009 things turned from bad to worse. One of our daughters went into a major meltdown, requiring hospitalization and many worrying months of appointments, treatment and juggling our lives. (To protect her, I am not going to identify her, nor give too many details. It will be her own choice whether or not she shares her story more widely when she is older.)

Our lives had to be completely reorganized around her needs and the impact on her sisters. Unusually I had a relatively quiet diary, and was able to drop everything – mainly because I had put time aside to write the earlier chapters of this book. Thankfully too, a recent change in Anne's anti-depressants had lifted some of the mist of anxiety and confusion from her mind, and she was able to cope with the massive reorganization of our lives.

We were sustained throughout by God's grace, by the emails and prayers of distant friends and family, and by practical help from many local friends. More than ten different families hosted one or more of our other daughters at weekends, so that we could give our full attention to our ill daughter. We never ate so much cottage pie or lasagne, quietly left on our doorstep by wonderful friends from church. In the circumstances, we asked no questions about the ethical sourcing of the meat!

Very slowly our daughter began to emerge from the crisis, helped by the clear routines, loving care and gentle counselling of experts (the NHS at its very best!), and by the unseen prayer of many others. Anne, meanwhile, was exhausted and fragile, but miraculously prevented from falling further into depression. I was also living on empty, emotionally, physically and spiritually, sustained by loving colleagues at work and church, by simply keeping my focus on one day at a time, and by holding desperately on to God, like a drowning man reaching for a lifebelt in a terrible storm.

Just as it seemed things were slowly improving, we suffered yet another setback. For the previous six months we had been living in temporary accommodation. The owner of our A Rocha housing had kindly offered to have the house completely refurbished, modernized and made more energy-efficient. London Diocese allowed us to use a nearby empty vicarage as a temporary home, but now our old house was ready and a new vicar needed to move in. So, in the midst of everything else, we were packing up, ready to move home.

It was mid-February. Anne was at home packing when she tripped while carrying a large box downstairs, and found herself in agony at the foot of the stairs. The paramedics thought she had broken one or both ankles, and she was whisked away for X-rays. It turned out that both ankles were severely sprained which, as medical friends seemed to delight in telling us, would probably take even longer to heal than if broken.

So we moved house, with Anne unable to walk, our children in various states of upset and confusion, and our lives feeling very much like all our stuff – a jumbled mess that made no sense. Again friends rallied round, unpacking, collecting children from school, making meals, and sometimes just being there to give a hug to anybody who needed it.

Shortly after moving, I was cycling back from taking the girls to school, thinking about how I had escaped from direct involvement in everything that was overwhelming the family, when suddenly a parked car flung open its door into my face, and I was thrown off my bike onto the pavement. I sat there dazed, with blood trickling down from my ear, as a small crowd gathered. The bike was almost untouched, as my head had taken the full force of the door. Once I recovered enough to stand up, a kind Muslim neighbour gave me a glass of water and walked me home, wheeling the bike. Anne took one look at me, and realized I needed to be checked out in hospital. So I became the latest Bookless in Casualty as I was examined for concussion, and damage to eyesight and hearing. Thankfully the messy head injury turned out to be only superficial, and I was quickly on the road to recovery.

Obviously Anne and I, along with praying friends, had been asking God what was going on and why. Was all of this simply coincidence – part of the consequence of living in a fallen world? Or were we, as we certainly felt ourselves to be, under some form of spiritual attack? Should we 'take authority' over the situation we found ourselves in and claim Christ's victory over the forces of darkness? Quite a number of friends felt that our prophetic message on creation and sustainability, the success of my book *Planetwise*, and A Rocha's growing influence, meant that God's enemy, the devil, was seeking to fight back. With others, we rebuked God's enemy, and prayed in detail for the whole situation, claiming the freedom that Jesus has already won through his death and resurrection.

At the same time, Anne and I both had a sense that God, the Divine Potter, might be using these painful events to mould and shape us into vessels that could glorify him more effectively. That is not to say that God sent or caused our daughter's illness, Anne's depression, sprained ankles or a bike accident. Far from popular opinion, God is never vindictive or cruel. He is always full of love and compassion. Yet neither does he always intervene when things go wrong. In the Old Testament story of Job, he allowed the devil to cause terrible disaster and personal suffering to his devoted follower. Chaos, suffering and sin are rampant, and often seem to go unchecked in the broken and damaged world in which we live.

Yet what we had discovered years earlier, with Anne's ME and our repeated miscarriages, proved to be true again in our experience. God does not cause suffering, but he can use it. If we turn to him in our pain, and offer our suffering to him, he is able to take it – to take us – and to transform us. It takes white-hot fire to refine gold and burn away the dross surrounding it. It needs the surgeon's knife, and the slow agony of chemotherapy, to remove the cancer from a diseased body. None of life's experiences, however brutalizing and crushing, however meaningless and random they may seem, need be wasted in God's plans. God who created from nothing can recreate from anything – however terrible it seems. God can recycle lost and broken people into new creations in Christ. God can also transform our most painful experiences into the labour pains of new life and new hope.

As Anne and I were reflecting on the first few months of 2009, and on our previous eight years with A Rocha UK, we also had an urgent practical decision to make. Two years earlier we'd agreed to speak at Lee Abbey together, and now the conference was fast approaching. Friends advised us to pull out, but we both had a strange feeling that, even in our broken state, we were meant to carry on. The title we'd given was 'Birdsong before Dawn', with the description: 'God's amazing creation contains light and dark, death and new birth, pain and beauty. So do our lives. Dave and Anne Bookless of A Rocha explore how God is at work in suffering and also in healing, in our Christian experience and in the wider natural world.'

We organized for each of the children to stay with trusted friends or family, and we drove down to Devon, still unsure about what we would say, and whether we would be able to speak without breaking down. In the end, the loving welcome of the community and the prayer that infuses Lee Abbey enabled us to share with complete openness about the wilderness we were going through.

We spoke of how we had wrestled with a good God who allowed terrible suffering, both in nature and in our own human experience, and yet how we tried to cling on to that God in the midst of the storm. There was a hushed silence and, as we talked to others in the breaks and at mealtimes, it was clear that God had gathered a very specific group of people for that weekend, including many deeply wounded individuals and couples, some of whom had experienced far worse suffering than us, and for far longer. Several had only decided to attend at the last minute, after a strong prompting that they 'just had to be there'. One or two couples included a partner who had lost their faith in God's love completely, due to tragedies they had experienced, but had come along out of loyalty, and found themselves profoundly touched by what we were able to share.

It felt as if all our painful experiences were no longer meaningless but, by being offered to God in all our vulnerability, they had somehow been transformed. We could echo Paul's words in Romans 8:28, that 'in all things God works for the good of those who love him, who have been called according to his purpose'. What seemed so negative had been shaped into something that reflected God's transforming presence. A conference on 'Birdsong before Dawn', singing God's praise in the time of greatest darkness, had seen the colours start to change on the eastern horizon.

Looking out at the beautiful Lee Abbey estate, with snowdrops appearing through the cold soil, and nesting seabirds returning to their ledges, it felt as if winter was ending, in more senses than one. We also realized again that, in God's economy and in his all-creative hands, nothing is ever wasted.

Nothing is wasted
(written in the aftermath of the Cumbrian floods of
November 2009)

Leaves fall and blow away,
Words cut and wound,
Attitudes fester within,
Seeds die and lie forgotten.
Relationships break like storm-hewn branches,
Long-dreamed plans unmade by illness or death,
Rivers of suffering overwhelm and break down bridges;
Run amok through fields leaving dirt and debris.
Potential lies wasted in a thousand damaged hearts.
Crops fail, islands sink, coral bleaches, ice melts;
Deserts creep forward relentlessly, smothering life and hope.
Death, the last enemy, always appears to win.

Yet this is not the end, the whole, the entire story.
Nothing need be wasted. Not one thing.

The mulch of decay and death give way to growth anew,
Bare soil sprouts green shoots.
The river that breaks banks can also cut new channels,
        spread fertile loam,
The canker of bitterness can ripen into the fruit of forgiveness,
Bridges can be rebuilt, stronger and more secure;
Stony hearts can be melted, icy faces warmed,
Deserts can bloom again.
The groaning of a dying creation gives birth to a new world.
One day a man returned from death,
And hope was vindicated,
The last enemy defeated;
Nothing wasted.
One day all things will be made new.
© Dave Bookless, 2009

Afterword: Unfinished

This book ends at a point where, both personally and in the growth of A Rocha UK, there are many loose ends. As I write, our daughter is back with us at home and at school full-time, receiving excellent professional support and continuing to feature in many people's prayers. She is unrecognizably happier than earlier this year. A few weeks ago I took her to the Lake District and together we climbed Scafell Pike, England's highest mountain. There is a joy about her now, and she has rediscovered her creativity.

Of course we simply do not know what the future holds for any of us. Anne continues to struggle with depression, and has stepped down from A Rocha to focus on the family and her health. I have reduced my travelling and national role, and become Director for Theology, Churches and Sustainable Communities, areas that I can focus on more from home. It has felt like stepping off the roller coaster of adventure and exhaustion that have summed up the A Rocha UK story. Yet it also feels right. It has enabled me to put down deeper roots again in my family, in my local church, and in the place that God has planted me. I am reminded that you can't be very fruitful unless you retain deep roots, and that applies socially and ecologically just as much as spiritually. Anne and I do not know what God has in store for us next. We continue to feel a deep passion for communicating the crisis that humanity has brought upon God's world, and also the hope that Christ gives for prayer-filled action. We try to remain open to whatever God wants, wherever and whatever in the world that might mean. And we try to offer everything that each day brings back to God, knowing that with him nothing is wasted. God doesn't do waste.

Notes

Chapter 1
1. 25 December 1916, in *The Collected Works of Mahatma Gandhi* (Government of India, 1958), p. 314.

Chapter 2
1. Quoted in: Dr Anna J. Brown, 'Roots, Reality and Religion: Simone Weil's Re-visioning of the World', July 2006, http://h06.cgpublisher. com/proposals/473/index_html.
2. Douglas Coupland, *Life After God* (New York: Pocket Books, 1995), p. 174.
3. Entry for 25 December 1916, in *The Collected Works of Mahatma Gandhi* (Government of India, 1958), p. 314.
4. Quoted by William Rees-Mogg in *The Times* (London, 4 April 2005).
5. An ashram is a spiritual community, often centred on a religious leader or teacher. The nearest Western equivalent might be a monastery or new monastic community. In India there are Hindu, Buddhist and Christian ashrams.

Chapter 3
1. *Bono on Bono: Conversations with Michka Assayas* (London: Hodder & Stoughton, 2005), p. 197.

Chapter 4
1. Transcribed from a talk given by Jean Vanier (Merville, France, September 2008).

Chapter 5
1. From *The Collection*, edited by Mark Elsdon-Dew (London: HTB Publications, 1996), p. 99.

Chapter 6
1. These words are spoken by British Asian Kiran to some Indians with a relative in Southall, and are in a 'Deleted Scene' on the DVD of *Bride and Prejudice*.
2. Jeremiah 29:11, *The Message*.

Chapter 7
1. *Three Cups of Tea* (Penguin, 2008), p. 112.

Chapter 9
1. Transcribed from a talk given by Peter Harris at A Rocha UK's 'Hope for the Planet' conference, St Michael's Chester Square, London, November 2005.

Chapter 10
1. 'Christianity and the Survival of Creation' from www.crosscurrents. org/berry.htm; also found in Wendell Berry, *Sex, Economy, Freedom & Community* (Pantheon Books, 1994).
2. Published in 2008 by Inter-Varsity Press.
3. Rob Frost, evangelist and broadcaster, died in November 2007.

Chapter 11
1. Quoted in John Lane, *Timeless Simplicity: Creative Living in a Consumer Society* (Green Books, 2001), p. 13.
2. John De Graaf, David Wann, Thomas H. Naylor, Scott Simon, and David Horsey, *Affluenza: The All-Consuming Epidemic* (McGraw-Hill, 2001) – the quote is from the book cover.
3. Rt Revd James Jones and Professor Sir John Houghton, 'Climate Change, Copenhagen and the United States: An Urgent Call to Prayer and Action', 9 November 2009.
4. John De Graaf, David Wann, Thomas H. Naylor, Scott Simon and David Horsey, 'Affluenza: The All-Consuming Epidemic', www.bookbrowse.com/reviews/index.cfm?book_number=884

Chapter 12
1. Archbishop of Canterbury's New Year message, 31 December 2007 (found in full at www.archbishopofcanterbury.org/1389).
2. Transcribed verbatim from a talk at Windsor Castle, May 2008.
3. From 'Stop Flapping and Start Belonging!' (*A Rocha UK Magazine*, February 2009), pp. 14–15.